Neighbors from Hell

Managing Today's Brand of Conflict Close to Home

by Bob Borzotta

Copyright © 1999-2009 by Robert Borzotta, Neighbor Solutions, LLC
ISBN: 1449582702
EAN-13: 9781449582708

All rights reserved. No part of this book may be reproduced or transmitted in any form or by any means, electronic or mechanical, including photocopying, recording, or by any information storage and retrieval system, without permission in writing from the copyright owner. Library of Congress control number pending.

This book was printed in the United States of America.

To order additional copies of this book, contact:
NFH@Borzotta.com

For specific guidance and further information, visit:
NeighborsFromHell.com

Dedication

I dedicate the Neighbors From Hell project – this book, the online materials and the guidance I give over the air – to Fred Rogers, whose fictional neighborhood and whose televised teachings to children encourage courtesy and empathy – two traits increasingly hard to find in the modern-day community.

Photo from Wikipedia

Acknowledgements

For 10 years, I've worked to make *Neighbors From Hell* come to life in print. Along this ride of ups and downs, research and rewriting, my wife Christine Brady has patiently read my work from a consumer's viewpoint, helping to ensure clarity within what is often complex and complicated material.

For several of those years, Uschi Johnson provided her moderating service to the NeighborsFromHell.com message board, keeping it spam-free and acting as an anchor for the tens of thousands of postings within this online support center. She passed away very young in 2009 and is quite missed.

Introduction: Home is Where the Heart *Was*

Most of us live among others in communities of various types, by choice or by necessity. We humans are naturally social creatures, but things can go wrong. And they do, and they have over the millennia, and disputes among neighbors are not a new concept. What is new, though, is an en-masse cultural shift away from neighborly behavior, timed most inconveniently with the turnabout in whose side is most likely to win – that of the *good* guy or the *bad* guy.

Not that long ago, a person complaining about his neighbor's noise got results. The system worked for someone who called the cops about the neighbor's barking dog or amplified music, after first trying to work face-to-face with the neighbors but with no acceptable results. The same went for other types of conflict close to home, from trash and pets to boundary disputes, from unsightly messes to threats and intimidation. Much has changed. There are now exponentially more things someone living in close proximity to others can do to annoy his neighbors, the laws that do exist are largely un-enforced, and the overall system designed to protect positive forces in the community – the good neighbors who *used to prevail* in such matters – is too taxed to deal with "petty neighbor squabbles," as police officers, judges, landlords, homeowners' association reps and countless others consider today's disputes.

The situation is further complicated by the fact that it's increasingly difficult to determine who's really at fault in some neighbor disputes. Is it the upstairs neighbor who walks across her bare floor while wearing shoes, or the downstairs neighbor who bangs on his ceiling in response? The woman with a constantly barking dog in a suburban community filled with dogs, or the next-door neighbor who eggs her house as retaliation for his sleepless nights? Is it the guy who some people think is staring at kids in the community, or the angry mob of parents who show up at his home with torches?

This is not your father's neighbor war. Welcome to the world of uphill, lonely battles that are more likely to send the good guy packing while the bad guy wins. I've lived rurally, in the suburbs, and in the city, in areas rich, middle-class and poor. I've counseled thousands of people online, over the airwaves and in person in dealing with the anxiety-filled force that now stands to change us at our cores and worsen our lives all around. I've experienced for myself most of what I cover in this book, and the rest is based on the outcomes of my counsel.

The forces stack against us. Good neighbors come and go while the bad ones never seem to move away or get swept up in a tsunami. Media messages over the last decade have bolstered bad neighbor behavior while marginalizing traditional "good neighbors" into what I call the Good Neighbor Underclass. Authorities, arbitrators, judges, and other *good* neighbors – all of whom could once be seen in our corner – now seem hasty in finding many of those who complain to be uptight, intolerant jerks who make their own problems and probably deserve the intense anxiety that their neighbors are causing.

I've quieted the loud, I've pushed back those who encroached against my boundaries, I've toppled the aggression of the Neighbors From Hell and all they employ in their childish, hateful campaigns. This fight is not for everyone, which is why I say:

There is a cost beyond the cover price of this book. Neighbor conflict takes a heavy toll, especially among good people who possess the growingly-unreasonable expectation that those around them will be equally neighborly. Good neighbors aren't built for war. We're positive people who have positive pursuits, and the negativity of neighbor-versus-neighbor challenges who we are. We focus in our lives on productive work – Neighbors From Hell are destructive and have more time to make us miserable than we have to correct them. They demonstrate an unquenchable thirst for conflict, while we're conflict-averse.

Today's neighbor wars pit good guys against each other – spouses fight, good neighbors wind up in conflict with authorities who we often see as siding with the bad neighbors (and we're often right), and we face an internal conflict at every stage, leading to what I call NFH Syndrome – where victims become aggressors, whether against their foils next door or against their families or themselves. Ask anyone who's been embroiled in neighbor turmoil for a year or two how he's sleeping, how she's handling her workload at the office, how their kids are doing in school with so little sleep because of overnight disturbances, how their bank account is fairing because they have to hire a lawyer to defend themselves against false claims, and how much they can enjoy a vacation while worrying what the Neighbors From Hell might do to their property while it's unprotected and the neighbors are unsupervised.

I've explored the multifaceted issues here, covering the major forms of neighbor disagreement, and I'll present my three-pronged approach of Prevention, Diplomacy and Correction toward returning your home and community life to normal –

Prevention – It may seem too late for that, but ongoing preventive measures are useful where we live now, and if you choose to move to a new home they can help you to *live where you belong*, in as much harmony as possible.

Diplomacy – This level is important because most of us don't approach a neighbor about a problem properly. We're too serious or too weak. We're angry and frustrated or we're frightened. We make the mistake of writing notes that can be used against us later by our Neighbors From Hell in a harassment claim. Unfortunately, diplomatic efforts typically expose us to *greater conflict* – we're effectively telling a troublemaker how he or she can cause us even more trouble. Kind of like shedding blood into a shark tank. It's the failure of diplomacy that yields for us the knowledge we are dealing with a bona-fide Neighbor From Hell. But diplomatic efforts can also yield a quicker resolution and even spawn a friendlier environment among neighbors that could become at odds.

Correction – Here is where I and thousands of others without proper preparation have found our greatest anxiety and frustration. There was a non-preventable problem, diplomacy did not work but only worsened things, and now we must engage police, lawyers, landlords, mediators, condo and co-op boards, local legislators, zoning and health officers, animal control and other agencies to work *for* us rather than *against* us. We also have to properly prepare ourselves for ongoing conflict so that it doesn't destroy us, malign us among our better neighbors, ruin our households and impact the well-being of people we care about.

Let me point out that once we reach the light at the end of the tunnel, we're not completely in the clear. Neighbors From Hell don't find God or any other salvation to become good neighbors once we prevail; friendships don't rise from the rubble left in the wake of our corrective efforts.

Neighbor conflict seldom goes away without one of the parties moving away or getting hit by a transit bus.

So our process continues as a matter of ongoing conflict management after the conflict resolution. We are, after all, the adults here. Embrace your new role as manager.

One of the major points that I press on NeighborSolutions.com, which offers a global support and information forum that anyone can join, is that beyond our individual issues with our own neighbors, I see from my research a cultural shift away from neighborly behavior and the erosion of community life as we know it. Where once proximity was likely to birth friendship, the term "neighbor" is for too many becoming a four-letter word. It's as though hate is being manufactured and sold to consumers on both sides – un-neighborly types hate us, and the Good Neighbor Underclass can do without the growing numbers of Neighbors From Hell.

But where can humanity go to avoid dealings with neighbors? There aren't enough islands to go around. I don't see people becoming more neighborly, so living NFH-free in today's society is more and more becoming a matter of careful choices, understanding of the issues of neighbor disputes, and knowing how to correct that which deserves our time and needs our attention.

Empathizing with those around us takes energy and may even curtail the extent to which we can enjoy ourselves. The way selfishness is eclipsing more neighborly attitudes is a sign we're losing touch with how to coexist in a community, which essentially predicts its eventual death. Life in the modern neighborhood is becoming a zero-sum game being won by the bad guys, sending nicer neighbors to flee for a peace that's now hard to find anywhere.

Most discouraging is that the good guys' suffering forces us to become something we weren't – defensive and combative, increasingly suspicious toward those around us, and looking up the neighborhood social ladder to see how far we've fallen.

Definitions, Statistics, and the Cast of Characters

Sometimes I think this book could just as easily be titled *The Nouveaux Trashe*.

That's my term for those not born into antisocial environs but who seem to abscond historically lower-class values, behaviors and personality traits for themselves. The nice thing about my term is that it doesn't demean people based on race, age, or any of the other no-no divisions we can draw – it's an equal-opportunity movement comprising people who are despicable for their behavior alone, a behavior that might fly in the face of their proper upbringing, but which they embrace nonetheless.

Some more terms:

Derelictometer: Veteran victims of Neighbors From Hell and *Entities* From Hell (see the Appendix) develop an unwanted talent for spotting derelicts. For instance, living near a nuisance bar, a homeowner can often tell when someone looking for a place to urinate is approaching, based on his shuffle and attempt to casually look around for a sufficiently secluded spot to unzip. Also, when new people are moving in, a neighbor watching them unload notices a number of things, from the items being moved in, to the general appearance of the new neighbors; if they seem to possess few furnishings but lots of stereo equipment, ATVs and more dogs than the local animal shelter, we know trouble lies ahead.

Good Neighbor Underclass: An underclass is a group of people it's okay to belittle, look down upon and mistreat. I've found that good neighbors, who once dominated the community and possessed a good deal of cultural clout, have in recent years been forming an underclass. This is demonstrated by a number of factors, including belittling by media messages and mistreatment by authorities.

Hippie-Wannabes: A younger generation of people today wishes to have been alive during the Age of Aquarius, its being so romanticized for fighting capitalism and war. They look and talk the part, but generally don't understand politics and economics because of slackened standards in school. They get their news from Comedy Central and left-leaning cable news outfits, so just give them a machine against which to rage and they'll go nuts.

> ***Neighbor From Hell***: After a decade of trying to refine a NFH "standard," I've found we each make up our own minds about defining what is hellish for ourselves. I can deal with lots of things you may not abide, while I can't stomach some of which you find acceptable.
>
> But then, simple is better, so here is my common-denominator definition of a ***Neighbor From Hell***: I begin with a good neighbor, and strip away all decency and maturity. Voila.

Neighbor Stupidity Curve: In early attempts at diplomatic resolution of a problem caused by a neighbor who's being loud, trespassing or committing some other act that offends or disrupts, we apply this curve to give him or her the benefit of the doubt. Perhaps he didn't realize that we can hear his acid rock at 3 a.m., blasting from a thin floor away; perhaps she wasn't aware that the plain-wood flower box on a wall separating our courtyards was mine long before she moved in, and that I don't want it painted a nauseating teal color. Applying the curve helps us in being pleasant with people who are outraging us with their behavior.

Noise Culture: Beyond nuisance noise itself is a social movement that compounds the original problem – how more and more loud neighbors are coming to respond to complainants. They've developed self-confidence unlike in the past, truly believing their way is the *right* way and that those who object are wrong and should be mistreated. This can be attributed to anti-neighbor influences flowing through our chief communications systems, influences that birth and rear noise culture. The entertainment industry and its marketing machinery increasingly present the noisy as part of a superior culture, one that's fun and funny and full of sexy people. Those who don't want to be disturbed are belittled in countless examples of noise culture media bolstering, which will be detailed further later.

Personality Type "NFH": Everyone's heard of Type "A" and Type "B" personalities – Type "NFH" is what makes Neighbors From Hell tick. Certainly, everyone's an individual, but Type "NFH" personalities share highly antisocial and often dangerous qualities, aimed more at those living in their midst than at non-neighbors. In fact, their behavior outside their homes and neighborhoods is inconsistent with the ill manners and strange affectations we come to know them for. Some are careful drivers, some are dedicated office workers. Awareness of this inconsistency is disturbing – wherever we go, we could easily be standing behind, driving alongside, or working for someone's Neighbor From Hell.

Premature Ingratiation: New neighbors who share too much personal information, too soon after meeting, are guilty of this. Steer clear of people who lack personal boundaries and gossip, and keep your private stuff private as well.

Venus Neighbor Trap: The plant of fantasy for NFH victims everywhere, it can be purchased at your local home gardening center for $39.95 and used to hedge yard boundaries, quickly devouring neighbors and others who trespass onto our property. In an age of livestock cloning and plant irradiation, there's no reason we can't have this.

NeighborSolutions.com and NeighborsFromHell.com are American-based sites, while serving the United Kingdom is a web presence called "NFHiB" – the "iB" standing for "in Britain." Our sites aren't connected beyond shared links and occasional communication amongst us, but I like to consider the sites "sisters" – good neighbors are good neighbors no matter the geography, and – that's right – bad neighbors exist well beyond U.S. shores.

In May 2006, NFHiB wrote up the results of an online survey. Here is their article:

Noise is top of neighbour from hell survey
A recent survey undertaken by the Neighbours From Hell In Britain (NFHiB) organisation, shows noisy neighbours as being the main source of Neighbour From Hell abuse in the UK. According to NFHiB, noise assault is clearly a serious problem in today's society, yet in comparison with other serious 'crimes,' it appears less action is taken by authorities to actually tackle the problem.

A spokesperson for NFHiB said: "Noise problems account for 21.82% of our survey. There are a lot of people who ignore their neighbours' rights to enjoy a peaceful, quiet life. There are clearly some Neighbours From Hell (NFH) who deliberately target neighbours with noise in order to harass or intimidate them."

NFHiB asked over 1,000 (1,077) people to give their views, ideas, information and facts concerning personal experiences with 'neighbours from hell' and almost 74% of people surveyed were experiencing current neighbour from hell problems. Surprisingly, 35% of survey participants did not know where they could get help to effectively tackle a nuisance neighbour.

When NFHiB asked if people felt things were generally better in their community now that ASBOs (Anti-Social Behaviour Orders) are in force and are being more commonly used, nearly 50% gave a thumbs down and felt the ASBO made no difference at all.

"It's hard for some people to believe this, but, here at NFHIB, we have plenty of evidence gathered from over 10,000 forum community members that this is what happens in many cases." When asked, most people turned to the Police or their Local Authority for help with a nuisance neighbour, closely followed by relying on friends/family for support. Over 40% of survey participants had used Neighbours From Hell in Britain as a source for help, advice and support.

Overwhelmingly, people want faster, more effective, practical action and response by the Police, the Courts and Local Authorities; they want these bodies to have better co-ordination, more communication and more powers/resources available to them. Those individuals living with a nuisance neighbour hugely agree that the whole process to deal with a neighbour from hell takes far too long, is incredibly frustrating and does not support the 'victim' positively, appropriately or successfully.

People feel powerless and vulnerable when on the receiving end of a neighbour from hell and more legal powers for those unwilling recipients of un-neighbourly behaviour should be available.

Causes of problems for neighbours were identified as being:
- Noise (21.82%)
- Anti-Social Behaviour (14.30%)
- Harassment (9.75%)
- Animal Disturbance (2.97%)

- Boundary Problems (4.27%)
- Car Parking Issues (or other vehicle problems) (4.27%)
- Children/Young People Problems (4.09%)
- Bullying (3.81%)
- 'Other' problems (2.88%)
- Rights of Way Issue (or shared access problem) (2.41%)
- General Garden related issue (0.84%)
- High Hedge Problem (0.84%)
- Rubbish/Litter (0.84%)
- Racism or other Hate Crime (0.46%)
- General Crime (0.19%)

The NFHiB spokesperson added: "Some NFH use a variety of deliberate methods to harass their neighbours. There have been cases of people playing loud music in the middle of the night, banging on walls, using power tools in the early hours of the morning, purposely blocking access to neighbouring properties, and so forth. Sadly, with some NFH there's no limit to what they will do, even sometimes to the extent of damaging property or using violence."

With the exception of the difference between how we spell "neighbor" and a few other words, my research concurs. That's why we're here. Let's meet the cast of characters ...

Us...
This story begins with the protagonists – the "good guys" – you, me, and our better neighbors. Some simply go about their lives without intentionally disturbing others, and some go out of their way to be great neighbors.

We have our wrinkles – good guys aren't 100 percent good. Non-dimensional characters are dull anyway, and we come with faults, foibles and shortcomings that can all contribute to our failures in dealing with the antagonists.

The good guys are decent people who tend to be law-abiding, empathetic, productive, and recognize the existence of a wide world around them. We're often maligned for complaining about others, and are increasingly judged by the world as the *real bad neighbors.*

Them...

The bad guys sometimes seem law-abiding, and their level of indecency is not easily recognizable to the general public (but we who live within an unsafe distance of them know the truth). Most I've studied have ambitions amounting to little more than taking up space and oxygen. Their level of empathy is low if it's there at all – selfishness and childishness more aptly describe their lifestyles, habits, ability to interact socially with others, and their manner of dealing with hearing their un-neighborly faults pointed out to them. Some are this way due to ignorance, and I've found many who see un-neighborly ways as a goal to shoot for.

I could devote all these pages to parsing the types and traits of good and bad neighbors and not cover every detail; the fact is, how hellish a situation is depends not only on them, but on us – our circumstances for one, and our ability to properly quash the un-neighborly among us for another.

I've worked with people whose neighbors were so hideous, they weren't satisfied with driving them to pack up and move, but felt the need to tail their moving van so they could learn their victims' new address in order to continue the harassment. Others have lost their homes to fire, still others have been hospitalized for assault, and a few have suffered emotional breakdowns so severe they required surgery (anxiety impacts every corner of the physical).

My point: Many of us can take some solace in knowing our own jerky neighbors aren't the world's worst. Let's avoid demonizing people for un-neighborly behavior – observe and judge them with some perspective, and you'll find taking them on much easier. Blow them up in your mind as a horrific force and you take the first step to losing the battle due to feeling overwhelmed.

…and the Authorities…

Sadly, the police become villains in many of these stories, even when their intentions began in our corner. It's difficult to arrive on the scene of interpersonal conflict and make an immediate call as to who's right and who's wrong, especially since bad neighbors know rather well how to hide their fangs when authorities come on the scene.

Police and other authorities generally seek compromise from both sides so that they can leave the scene with a feeling that the parties are now going to either act constructively and positively, or will at least stay away from each other.

We good neighbors tend to rob the cops and others of this feeling of accomplishment, because we don't buy into the idea set forth by our nasty neighbors that they will become better neighbors. *Compromise* prescribed by police – over noise levels, dog-do, harassment and other issues – comes down upon us as a *punishment,* one administered to us despite the fact we are right and usually are the ones who called the authorities in the first place, seeking justice. But justice for the Good Neighbor Underclass does not come that easily.

When we don't capitulate to compromise, it puts us and police at odds. They determine we're unreasonable because we won't compromise, making them feel ineffective. The bad neighbors, meanwhile, emerge in the eyes of many authorities as the more reasonable party; this is easy when you were causing the trouble in the first place, and you're not being completely quashed. It isn't just the police who seek our unpalatable compromise, but condo board members, other good neighbors, zoning officials, landlords and anyone else not standing in our precise shoes.

There Goes the Neighborhood
Stories from the Front

The neighborhood has changed. Simple differences among people living in close proximity are now more common occurrences, and are more difficult to address. They typically snowball from simple matters into complicated messes, and seem impossible to resolve as they persist for years, eating away at home life – sometimes for people on both sides.

There's more to complain about now than ever before. The barking dog has become the vicious dog. Loud music has become a bass-enhanced, earth-shaking experience that forces everyone around the reveler to partake in his taste in music, movies and talentless guitar practice. Boundary disputes are becoming much more complicated, as fencing issues pale by comparison to those created by shared driveways, shining lights and surveillance cameras. Are neighborhood kids just as bad now as they always were? Let's put it this way: Did they always videotape their antics from vandalism to "beat-downs" of other kids to post them on YouTube?

So many of us no longer live in community-centric neighborhoods, be they within the city, the suburbs or a rural area, so *we are now less likely to know our neighbors by name*. We don't seek friendships in our own backyards, choosing instead the long-distance relationships established over time, sustained via email and low-cost telephone conversations. When we don't know the people living adjacent to us, we tend to assign to them the traits we learn about the outside world from the local news and reality shows. So, before getting to know our neighbors, we're quick to determine they're vacuous, insensitive wannabes. And they have been taught by media influences we are intolerant, uptight jerks who deserve their harassment.

While every generation can say the world's gone to hell, referring to the generation in tow, there indeed have been social changes and movements away from neighborly behavior. The evidence is everywhere – in the news, in police logs, and in the ever-growing number of people registering with NeighborSolutions.com and writing to me for help. Every other day I come across a news story that has something to do with this subject. Some make me happy ...

```
CANTON, Ohio (AP) - June 3, 2008 --
Homeowners who don't mow their grass in this
```

```
          Northeast Ohio city now face stiffer
          penalties - including possible jail time.
             The city council unanimously passed a law
          Monday that makes a second high-grass
          violation a fourth-degree misdemeanor
          carrying a fine of up to $250 and as many as
          30 days in jail.
             The previous law only made the first
          violation a minor misdemeanor, with a fine of
          up to $150 but no jail time. The new law is
          to take effect in 30 days.
             "This is the type of action we need to take
          in order to clean up our neighborhoods and
          our city," Mayor William J. Healy II said.
             The laws are an effort to reduce the
          roughly $250,000 the city spends to cut about
          2,000 private lots each year and to address
          public complaints, Councilman Greg Hawk has
          said.
```

But most times, I read woeful entries on the NFH message board, and see the long list of neighbor noise calls in the police logs, and come across news and other media content that demonstrates how bad off we of the Good Neighbor Underclass really are.

And these come as no surprise, since I've experienced it all for myself first-hand.

The Roaches

As a child I lived beside motorcycle-riding hoodlum teens who revved and rode all around a vacant lot beside my parents' house, all day and all night. My parents ultimately moved to a rural area where sheep were our neighbors (dull, but quite peaceful). During college I lived with my girlfriend below a roofing contractor who I nicknamed the Fat Beer-Guzzling Moron. Heavy-footed, door-slamming, hard-partying and ugly, he epitomized the term I personally find offensive for the same reason blacks find the N-word offensive: white trash.

So in 1993 when I purchased my home in Philadelphia I probably should have expected to be revisited by the scourge of bad neighbors, but still didn't realize they were multiplying faster than the good. My initial neighbors were fantastic, but as stated earlier, good neighbors move away or die. Bad ones grow roots like crab grass.

The Roaches (not their real name) did just that. They were initially noisy and got noisier, after I brought their disturbance to their attention. They later keyed my car, filled my townhouse with smoke from their below-code chimney, and engaged in a public relations battle to get the neighborhood against me.

The Roaches taught me the most important aspects of noisy Neighbors From Hell. At the time I focused on the fact they were *hippie wannabes* who viewed me as a conservative cross between Bill O'Reilly and Rush Limbaugh – a machine against which to rage (mainly because I dress well for work and have a job). Their tie-dyes and ironic military fatigues (why do anti-military militants wear them?), their inescapable music wafting through the brick that separated our historic homes, their anti-establishment ways – for a while I was convinced all liberals are bad neighbors. (And they're not.)

But none of that really mattered. In studying them the way a scientific researcher studies animals in the wild, I determined where they were weak and attacked them in those areas. More on that later.

Mimi Cass

Although I'm born and raised in New Jersey, I've spent my whole adult life in Philadelphia and its suburbs. When my wife and I decided to start a family, we moved to South Jersey for the space, the schools and its closeness to the city.

We've learned that while Philadelphia has its problems – from a high murder rate to political corruption to trouble finding a place to park – the People's Republic of South Jersey is much less livable. In fact, I believe that the craziest street person in Philadelphia has better social skills than many an over-caffeinated soccer mom in South Jersey driving a schoolbus-sized SUV, and I'm not kidding. You can actually converse with some homeless people in the city, while many suburban moms can be just downright frightening. My wife and I have now started our family, and we're heading back to Philadelphia.

Mimi Cass is so-named because her first name is indeed Mimi, while I added the fictitious last name in honor of Mama Cass, a rather heavy singer who sang great songs until she choked on a ham sandwich and died. My neighbor Mimi, in response to my request that she not leave her barking dog out all night, not allow her kids to throw eggs and rocks at my house, and not build her fence over the boundary of our properties, *started to sing*. And she belts out a tune every time she sees me now. We'd previously been friendly enough with each other, but then I had the audacity to make that request.

Mimi Cass enjoyed the status of having been a long-time resident in a town where – despite its close proximity to Philadelphia (10 minutes from Center City), many people here had never crossed the bridge. It's an insular place that doesn't take kindly to having its faults pointed out, just as bad neighbors don't want to hear our complaints.

So it came as little surprise that local police officers and sergeants, called in after I'd spent nearly a year trying without success to get Mimi Cass to comply with our wishes and the law, provided no help. It didn't matter that they could hear her dog barking and it was after the legal limit of 10 p.m.; it didn't matter that she and her friends were using their vehicles to harass us with horn-honking. All that mattered to police was that Mimi Cass cried – officer sympathy goes a long way in neighbor dispute cases. I don't cry and I won't fake it.

I repeatedly emphasize the importance of maintaining healthy social interactions throughout our neighborhoods, as this reduces the chance for neighbor disputes to occur and boosts the chance for small differences to be worked out. But here we have an example of how things can go bad, despite there having been a positive relationship at first.

Mimi Cass came after the Roaches in my personal NFH experience, so I knew to be concerned when we moved in and she said her cute, small dogs "sometimes bark" and that one evening a neighbor knocked on her door and yelled at her about it; with my background I knew then and there how likely it was her dogs had been barking endlessly, late at night, for many nights before that neighbor would have visited her. She referred to herself as "an old hippie" and gave us a little front-yard sign that said "Welcome Friends."

Sadly, the traditional gestures and friendliness we used to find welcoming now need to be suspect. My wife didn't agree with this, at first. Mimi Cass exhibited signs I recognized as *overcompensation*. She knew living beside her posed challenges to any neighbor, so she set out early in our relationship to establish herself as a nice person, a giving neighbor, someone we'd hate to have to bring a complaint to. Bad neighbors can be good at manipulation.

Just to clarify – pleasantness, kindness, even a welcome basket can all be nice things exchanged between new neighbors. I'm not saying don't offer them, and I'm not saying that when they're offered to us we're dealing with a bad neighbor who's overcompensating. These days, I'm sorry to say, gestures beyond friendliness such as gifts might raise a red flag. What is expected in return for the gift?

Moreover, when you regale me with personal information about yourself that should have stayed personal, when you gossip to me about other neighbors you don't like, I consider this *premature ingratiation*. We've just met. If you're as blind to physical boundaries as you are to your personal ones (or mine), I'm figuring I need to get price quotes for a 10-foot fence.

It wasn't long before Mimi's dogs, barking from their backyard right up into our closed bedroom window, for hours sometimes, often through the evening, and sometimes during overnight hours, warranted a little talk with their owner. Cynical as I am about diplomacy ever working with a noisy neighbor, I always have and always will give it a shot. I started with face-to-face discussion; when that predictably didn't solve the problem, I wrote her a note (before knowing notes get used against you by Neighbors From Hell). The hellos stopped, and when the first note didn't work, I wrote her a less pleasant note, threatening to file police complaints about the nuisance noise; when that predictably didn't work, I called the cops.

I had extended to Mimi much more patience regarding her barking dog noise than I would have if she weren't pitiful. Having become grossly overweight during the last few years, she suffered a nasty consequence: her husband, a doctor, left her and their two pre-teens for his younger, slimmer secretary. That sucks. We knew her whole sad story the first time we met. The estranged husband complains about paying her alimony and child support, she drinks herself to sleep, she is chronically stricken by cold and flu – and while all this makes her pathetic, it doesn't justify her un-neighborly behavior. If I seem insensitive to her plight now, it's because I allowed it to lengthen the time between the start and end of her nuisance noise.

Diplomacy and involving authorities didn't work. What else is new? Time for Plan B.

Pathetic or not, Mimi's days of disturbing the peace in and around my home were now going to end. For her, staying up way past midnight on a Friday, letting her dogs bark to wake the neighbors, meant wanting to enjoy a little shut-eye the next morning.

Since I didn't want to disturb the rest of the neighborhood, I needed to contain Mimi's 5:45 a.m. Saturday wake-up call to her home. So I simply knocked on her door and rang her bell at that early hour. Then I walked away. Her dogs, inside for the overnight and early morning hours, went wild. I heard their indoor barking continue as I returned to my front door. There was no sleeping through it. Now, just as bad neighbors seem to like when we react to their bothers, whether we yell out our windows or call the police, I enjoy the same type of feedback as a member of the Good Neighbor Underclass. I wanted confirmation she'd been disturbed.

Police officers showed up later that day at my home to give me that confirmation. Wow, what service Mimi gets – I complain for a dozen consecutive Friday and Saturday nights over the course of months, asking for their help in the matter, even filing a police complaint against Mimi, and cops don't pay her any personal visit. I make one early-morning knock on her door (having checked whether there was any law against that, and there wasn't) and two big guys with guns come to see me. I guess I'm not as good at playing the damsel in distress.

Now, there's a police term about complaints phoned in that can't be substantiated when an officer arrives on the scene and the reported crime doesn't appear to be taking place. It's "unfounded" when the patrol car window gets rolled down outside the home of a neighbor we've reported for noise, and no noise is evident to the officer in the car. He or she radios back to the dispatcher that the complaint is unfounded, which means the caller and his phone number are flagged as having made a complaint that could not be substantiated.

And, while the term "unfounded" applied if officers didn't hear Mimi's dogs barking after midnight, it somehow doesn't come in to play when cops show up and *don't see me outside her door, knocking.*

I knew the officers personally, so they were not as nasty to me as they'd be to other members of the underclass who finally defended themselves against an aggressive noisemaker in the neighborhood. And many cops treat noise complainants much worse than they treat the source of the complaint. However, they did let me know I can't knock on her door anymore, that I would be charged with harassment if I did.

So, to recap, she can disturb my sleep at night when it's illegal to make nuisance noise, but I can't disturb her sleep in the morning by knocking on her door, which is not illegal.

No matter. Mimi now knows I will match her disturbances with my own. I've continued the measure as much as needed, throwing caution to the legal wind in town. Her barking dogs have been brought in by around 10 most nights since then. She likely thinks she showed me up by having the police come to see me, but all she really showed me was that my plan to fight fire with fire worked.

Her calling the police proved to me I could disturb her just as easily as she can disturb me. For that, she has my gratitude.

Dirty Girl and Huggy Bear

My last neighbors in Philadelphia should have convinced me not to live in Philadelphia ever again. But they were, in fact, from South Jersey.

Dirty Girl and Huggy Bear were lousy neighbors, and would have been lousy neighbors no matter where they'd come from. Dirty Girl was the privileged daughter of upper-income-earning Jerseys, so she never had to work and could instead focus on building a career that would never happen in the music industry. These were loud neighbors to be sure and I won't bother to describe their parties in detail, their talentless bass guitar playing or the pounding up and down their bare stairs in wooden shoes beside my townhouse.

I mention her, and her young boyfriend I nicknamed Huggy Bear because he dressed and looked like the Starsky & Hutch character (although he was actually white and young) – to make a point. As the web designer for local rock radio stations I had connections that could have helped my young neighbors in their endeavors. After all, what sounds like stupid child's play musically to me could be quite a hit among the masses – I'm nothing if not blissfully detached from popular culture.

But rather than getting to know me, being polite and saying hello, they chose to shun the adult neighbors of the adult world their parents had bought them into, making all kinds of noise from their post-noon wake-up through their overnight partying. They ensured I'd never consider doing anything for them, the way neighbors once helped each other with everything from a cup of sugar to a job lead.

So Dirty Girl, so named by me for her alley-cat appearance (ugly clothing and just-woke-up/just-beaten-up hairdo) despite her purebred upbringing, won't soon get a shot at impressing the DJs and club owners I know.

Lesson: Better neighbors have a bounty of good things to give their neighbors, and we give them, but discriminately. The good we withhold from bad neighbors is in many ways the equivalent of inflicting harm upon them, a consolation and even a form of ammunition for the Good Neighbor Underclass.

A Sad Ending

One story I feel compelled to mention up top did not involve me directly, but I came to know some of the players early in my reporting career. I came across a local matter that didn't seem initially like a neighbor story, but my news reporting background and growing sense of the expanse of neighbor conflict told me this was up my alley. The local morning TV news said a warehouse converted into condos was burned completely in a fire caused by careless smoking.

The careless smoker, it turns out, was the Neighbor From Hell for everyone in a building rife with neighbor disputes over noise, parking, pet issues, and weird stuff that included someone's life-like doll collection being stood up in common hallways and elevators. *Everybody hated everybody.* Police had been involved, but left resolution to the condo association, which was poorly organized and toothless in its power. Police often defer to homeowners associations in neighbor disputes, claiming management has jurisdiction in such matters and, in some cases, that they have none.

(That's horse manure. If one neighbor kills another, the police have jurisdiction, and that's the same with any law on the books. Police, as will be fully explored later, prefer to steer clear of neighbor disputes if at all possible. It's nice for a city or town to collect tax dollars and not have to involve itself in neighbor dispute resolution, and I see this more with condos, co-ops and gated communities than anywhere else.)

The guy who destroyed everyone's home had dozens of police complaints against him, and a handful of letters from management instructing him to "keep it down," coining the ultimate impotent phrase of any disinterested authority in dealing with a noisy Neighbor From Hell.

He'd thrown his drugged-up girlfriend out one night, leading to a drama for the entire community to endure at 4 a.m. He'd once threatened to kill his upstairs neighbor for spying on him with surveillance equipment, and for making too much noise (it always interests me when a noisy neighbor complains himself about someone making too much noise).

And that night, this loser awoke on his smoldering couch and attempted to put out the fire with – don't you know – a bottle of vodka. He then went running from the building without bothering to disturb any of his neighbors from their overnight sleep (the one wake-up they might not have minded), and has since left the country. It took four years for the building to get completely repaired and rebuilt, and many homeowners had to let their mortgage companies foreclose on their properties since their insurance policies only paid one year's worth of mortgage payments, and these folks had to continue to pay to live elsewhere while their burned-out homes were caught up in red tape and reconstruction issues. Lesson: Noisy neighbors can bring much more than a nuisance-type disturbance to those living nearby.

Section I.

The Issues

Chapter 1: Noise – In the Ear of the Beholder
The cultural shift away from neighborly behavior and empathy

I'm listening to news radio in my car and I hear a sad story about a young woman who was killed while jogging, when a tree limb fell on her. In typical fashion, the reporter aired a sound bite from a neighbor. That neighbor said, "She was so nice, she never complained about noise or nothing."

And I think to myself, when did things get so twisted in our communities that "she never complained about noise" came to replace "she never *made* noise"?

It's not that the quote shocked me. I'd already been researching the subject and dealing with it in my personal life for more than a decade. Advertisements, the entertainment industry and the media in general have seemingly conspired to usher in an age of *noise culture*, and it's taken over.

In a pop-media culture, society's ruling class is determined by advertisers, so noise culture's being crowned as the king for reaching the sought-after young demographic means the popularization of all things noisy, making nuisance noise a widespread norm that calls on the rest of us to accept it. Nuisance noise is the one form of neighbor conflict actually being worsened and perpetuated by current popular trends.

Not every piece of media content supports the idea that noisiness is next to godliness, but here are a few examples of messages that stand to impact neighbor behavior and general perceptions of complainants:

- A TV cola ad showed two soda delivery truck drivers – one Coke and one Pepsi – side by side, staring each other down at a stop light as though they're about to drag-race. The Coke guy turns up his music really loud and gives his foe a competitive grin. The Pepsi guy outdoes him – he throws a few switches and the truck opens up to expose concert-venue speakers that pound the surrounding air with bass, while the truck bounces up and down and young onlookers nod approvingly and sway to the beat. When the Pepsi driver departs, the Coke driver left behind admits, "That was awesome."
- Advertisements in magazines aimed at teens and twenty-somethings belittle neighbors for complaining about the noise of their bass-

25

boosted stereos and talentless guitar practice. One shows a young man in shades with messy hair giving the finger to the camera with a confrontational look on his face, beneath the ad's headline, "Turn It Down? I Don't Think So." Smaller print reads, "Not You. Not On Your Turf. Not With Boss Audio Systems." Notice the "turf" reference, empowering readers to make noise that in fact *leaves* their turf. Stereo speaker ads for the car and the home are particularly offensive to peace-seeking neighbors; one from JBL reads, "Either We Love Bass or <u>Hate</u> Your <u>Neighbors</u>" (their emphasis, not mine). Imagine an ad for an upscale men's club that reads, "Either We Love Cigar Smoke or Hate Our Wives." Or, since loud neighbors are encouraged to essentially torture neighbors, how about a tobacco ad that shows a smoker burning a non-smoker with his lit cigarette, with a "No Smoking" sign in the background? Messages assailing good citizens who complain about their neighbors' noise habits are okay, though, because no protected class is getting hurt.

- A Snoop Dogg film featured him greeting police during a party in his apartment, who say they'd received complaints about the noise. He says okay to the officers, slams the door on them, then orders his fellow partiers, "Turn that up." The scene was used in trailers and TV ads. Does it reflect the way some people react to police orders to hush? Usually. Does it plant a seed in those who'd previously possessed a degree of respect for authority, a seed that may grow into the same disrespect Snoop exhibits?

- Almost twenty years ago, Jay Leno sold Doritos in TV ads with the tag line, "Eat all you want, we'll make more." A 2003 ad for Doritos that ran in the United Kingdom showed Kelly Osbourne, offspring of the now brain-dead but still successful rocker Ozzy, playing loud music in her apartment. The downstairs neighbors are disturbed and want it to stop, but one says, "I don't want to be the jerk from downstairs who complains about the noise." He finally knocks on her door and is greeted by Ms. Osbourne munching on Doritos; he politely asks her to keep it down. An off-camera voice shouts from within Osbourne's flat asking who's at the door, to which she responds, "Oh, just some jerk from downstairs complaining about the noise."

- The 2005 Volkswagen Jetta ad campaign targeted twenty-somethings stuck between pre-adulthood and maturity. A young and very hip couple is blasting "Molly's Chambers" by the Kings of Leon while stomp-dancing in their apartment above an older neighbor, who comes by to complain. In the next scene, they're driving in their new Jetta with recently purchased, huge, powerful speakers visible in the backseat; they're evidently planning to really blow that complaining neighbor away with much worse sound than he could have imagined. The ad closes with the couple stomp-dancing once again to the bass of their new equipment. The shot zooms out and we learn they've moved into a single home with no one below, and the Jetta sits in the driveway. Despite the relief we can then feel for the poor neighbor below them, the message was still clear – exacting revenge against complaining neighbors is good fun – the right thing to do and worth the investment.

- In 2007, HGTV aired an episode of "What's With That House?" about unusual housing, and in one segment, a couple tore down a bungalow in a neighborhood filled with bungalows to build a large modern home. I was interested because I'm a fan of modern residential architecture. The show, hosted by a 20-something guy with bleached white hair and a tuft of white hair above his chin (whose overtly cool look is completed by his chic glasses), highlighted a neighbor difficulty during construction. Construction noise had disturbed a neighbor to the point where he turned his hose on the homeowner. The young host laughed and joked about the event. The homeowner said his contractor went and attacked the guy physically. Later in the segment, when looking into a composting can, the host joked again about the noise-disturbed neighbor, saying he was in there, decomposing, for having responded to the construction noise. We don't know details, but let's assume he was knocked to the ground and threatened, or merely lectured, by the construction noisemaker and his contractor about not getting them wet when they're trying to make noise (and I do consider construction noise -- within limits -- to be indicative of positive things happening in a community, unlike unnecessary obnoxious noise from any number of sources). Must the oh-so-cool host joke that the noise complainant was killed? Did others involved in the show have to keep all of that stuff in? It had nothing to do with the modern architecture that I, as a viewer, was interested in seeing. To me, it was HGTV's way of jumping on the old noise culture media bandwagon. Not only did this show tell me I'm unwanted as a viewer, despite belonging to the renovation demographic they want watching so they can sell advertising to Home Depot, but it told all the other viewers THEY ARE WRONG to ever complain about noise. I haven't watched that show again.

- In 2009, David Letterman was interrupted while doing his show by his "next-door neighbor," a guy who, the bit goes, lives right beside Dave's studio audience. He said, "I don't wanna be *that guy* (using air-quotes), but …" and then proceeded to complain about the noise from the band. It's a funny enough concept that there's someone living beyond the double doors of the studio, but it needed a little edge. So the guy then says he's going to kill the show's announcer if he's disturbed again. I realize it's in the name of comedy, and I laughed myself, but it's another example of

        unflattering portrayal of people who
        complain about neighbor noise.

It's not a real media conspiracy, of course, and it isn't even personal. It's business. When you're selling stuff to not-so-smart people, you need to know what they like. They like noise. It doesn't matter if you're selling Pepsi or Volkswagens, you portray happy, sexy people drinking Pepsi and driving Volkswagens, and show it in an antisocially noisy setting once you learn consumers seem to like that sort of thing. The non-Pepsi drinkers and non-Volkswagen drivers are meanwhile unappealing and unsatisfied with life, since it's too noisy.

Even if such messaging didn't induce misbehavior toward people living in close proximity, it certainly boosts the morale of the noise-acculturated as they endure complaints from the rest of us. It keeps them strong in their will, because they know from the messages that they are part of the prevailing culture. We who want peace and quiet are from another time – out of the zeitgeist.

No, there's no conspiracy, but there might as well be. The majority of people being sheep-like, they do as they're told. Either they embrace and enjoy the noise for its purported social benefits, or at least put up with it so as not to join those unappealing, miserable folks who find it distasteful. After a few years of en-masse media popularization of noise culture, you find growing numbers of people who just *love* a neighbor who never complained about noise or "nothing."

Not long ago, if you complained about a neighbor's noise, you'd get results. Today you get ridiculed.

Welcome to the Good Neighbor Underclass. Aggressive neighbor nuisance noise has become the number-one complaint people have about those living nearby. The problem is so resolvable, yet to the great frustration of millions and myself, it isn't getting resolved now or any time in the near future.

It's an easy enough problem to solve because in most cases it could be ended by calling the police, who can write costly tickets to offenders, who generally cannot afford to pay ongoing penalties for their antisocial sounds.

But it's the most difficult to solve because that seldom happens. Despite local and state governments being strapped for cash, authorities empowered to quash neighbor noise through ticketing and other measures, *don't*. Many police and political leaders say they *can't*. I say they *won't*. More on that later.

Noise disagreements between neighbors seldom get resolved easily or permanently, and typically bring with them years of anxiety as the situation snowballs. Dare to tell the wrong person not to play basketball beneath your bedroom window at midnight, or to bring Rover in after 10 p.m., or to put an end to the garage band of talentless teens, and you'll find yourself engulfed in a war wrought with misery, lawyers, harassment and the utter loss of enjoyment in and around your home. Emotions run so high among the noise-acculturated that traditional, peace-seeking neighbors seem outnumbered, and their safety has been put at serious risk in more cases than you'd think.

Many noisy neighbors feel we're giving them directives as to how they must behave in and around their own homes. In a sense, they're right, when what they do in their homes affects us, especially in a dense mini society such as a community of clustered housing. But a key component that should come with subwoofers, drum sets, leaf-blowers and barking dogs is missing: Empathy. It wasn't in the box. Empathy is sold separately and seems a less likely consideration for many consumers than the superfluous warranty. Although the paramount golden rule of neighborly behavior remains doing unto others and so forth, many people treat the concept as passé because it's simply not self-serving. If making disruptive noise equals pleasure, then to hell with the neighbors. Most noisy neighbors know better than to behave as they do, but fun-lust eclipses their sensibility. It somehow falls to the better neighbors of the world to force them to regain their senses. And moving against the tide of noise-acculturated Neighbors From Hell is no easy feat.

Nuisance noise is widely considered in New York City to be the worst aspect of city living, its aggravation focused sharply on neighbors due to almost all living spaces there being clustered. In October 2002, the *New York Times* reported on the city's revitalized aggressive approach to dealing with nuisance noise, called by the Bloomberg Administration "Operation Silent Night."

```
Yesterday (October 2), Mayor Bloomberg
announced a program to tackle the quality-of-
life problem most vexing to New York City
residents — barking dogs, screeching car
alarms, hideous music blaring from cars and
drunken bar patrons who share their feelings
with everyone on a block at 3 a.m. The
initiative, known as Operation Silent Night,
is the city's most aggressive attack on noise
since 1994, when the Police Department went
```

> after noisemakers, particularly in Greenwich Village in Manhattan, with summonses.
>
> ... Of the 97,000 complaints that come into the [three-digit quality-of-life hot line] each year, about 85 percent are about noise. Already in 2002, 93,000 New Yorkers have called with complaints about excessive or disruptive noise. Further, the city has hired consultants to help rewrite the city's noise laws, which have not been updated since 1972.
>
> Noise complaints that come into the quality-of-life hot line, or to police precincts or the Department of Environmental Protection, will now be fast-tracked to each precinct's executive officer, who will be responsible for addressing the complaint quickly. The police will work with city agencies to enforce the laws.

It took seven years for cities like Philadelphia to introduce their own non-emergency police help lines, but progress does happen. Police are increasingly expected to aid in resolving neighbor disputes, but these are usually not simple matters that need only a wave of an officer's magic nightstick to make the problems go away. And, occasional press about good guys winning succeeds at keeping the good guys satisfied, despite the trend I find everywhere I look, that such initiatives are short-lived and need to be kept alive by the Good Neighbor Underclass; however, as I keep saying, we're focused on the positive in life and rarely devote ourselves to policing the police who are telling us how much they're helping us.

Noise Culture Attitudes

Today, many feel booming-bass cars and home-theater systems, yapping dogs, screaming children, fireworks and high-pitched leaf blowers all make up the landscape of ordinary sounds of life, and the only noise they *don't want to hear* is that from complainants and good-neighbor advocates. Consider some of the hate mail sent to the NoiseFree.org web site for Noise-Free America – a group advocating substantiation and enforcement of noise laws (these are presented as written by adoring fans):

- > what the hell do you think your doing you worthless son of a bitch. thats the gayest thing ive ever seen in my life. if i find

out where you live ill personally move in right behind you and get the biggest stereo ever and blast it 24/7 you are worthless. you are an embaressment to our country, thats why people think USA is pussys is because of little fags like yourself
- Im tired of you whiny little fuckers whining about every little thing that makes "too much noise". Are you aware that louder motorcycles are safer???? Most people do not look for motorcyclists like my self. The only thing that keeps me from being killed by some dumbfuck is the fact that my Harley is LOUD ENOUGH FOR PEOPLE TO HEAR ME. And if you dont like it... TOO FUCKING BAD!!! Do you realise that the sound of those "loud" Harleys is a 100 year old tradition??? That sound is as fucking american as apple pie and napalm.
- THANKS TO YOUR NEED TO CONTROL OTHERS MY SON HAS JUST RECIEVED 5 DAYS IN JAIL AND FORMAL PROBATION FOR SIX MONTHS. THIS WAS HIS FIRST NOISE TICKET, ISSUED AT 5:32PM IN A BUSINESS AREA, FROM A STOCK STEREO. I HOPE IN THE FUTURE YOU ALL ARE SUBJECT TO SOMEONE ELSES \"NO TOLORENCE LAWS\" AND YOU SPEND TIME IN JAIL AND THAT YOU MUST BE SUBJECT TO ARREST AND SEARCH AT ANY MONENT.
- *(The following was submitted to the site in March 2003 by Terry McKenney, a member of the Maine State Legislature:)* After visiting the web site of the organization you purport to represent I am elated that there is no chapter in Maine. The Draconian measures advocated would be better suited to the era of the Salem witch trials or might make good reading as a futuristic science fiction novel.
- Yes, there will be a day when there will be no loud motor cycles, stereos, concert venues, neighbors, or anything else. The day you die.

    From such expressions we glean insight into the mind of very bad neighbors, embodied by noise, trashy attitudes and selfishness.

    That potentially dangerous mind is yet another factor that weakens our credibility when we decide to knock on the neighbor's door when he or she is too loud. People with such animosity toward noise complainants may seem to be in the minority, but just one next-door neighbor who feels justified in harming those intolerant of nuisance noise is all it takes, if he's next door to you.

I was a guest on a live call-in show in New York City when a woman called in with the story of her friend's murder at the hands of a handyman to whom she'd complained about his noise. He was working in an adjacent apartment, she came by to complain about the noise, and he followed her back to her place and beat her to death.

The noise-acculturated have learned that we who complain *deserve* retaliation – the ads and movies leave it at belittling or upping the volume, but the line drawn for less intelligent people is unclear.

Perhaps no other type of neighbor problem, be it trespassing, squalor or pet issues, is actually *worsened* by current popular culture and its media influences, the way noise is. Those who expect traditional neighbor values about keeping it down have become subject to ridicule and, more and more, seem to be in harm's way.

Noise culture is gaining such momentum that it looms as a potential 21st century American melting pot – the singular brand of assimilation that can survive as diversity agendas and disparity celebration have hung the old pot on the rack. The Good Neighbor Underclass is unprotected; it's okay for traditional-minded neighbors to be harassed. After all, the media messages championing noise culture and embracing trashy attitudes say so.

Innocence among "good" and "bad" neighbors

It's important to note that anyone can be a noisy neighbor without the intent of harming others in their midst. I personally probably played my music too loud when I first bought my small townhouse in Philadelphia, playing the stereo while I did my renovation work. No one ever spoke with me about it, so I knew of no problems I was causing. But with the perspective I have today, I figure I *was* disturbing adjacent neighbors, but they chose not to confront me about it.

If they had, I would have lowered the radio volume. There's not much one can do about hammers and power tools – they don't have volume buttons. They can and should be used only within reasonable hours, which are typically stipulated by municipal law.

Many of us consider ourselves utterly innocent of making too much noise, even though our lives can make sounds that could bother others living nearby. It seems to me that only after we've been truly disturbed by a neighbor's noise and have had no luck in resolving the issue with the neighbor face-to-face, and then through authorities, can we appreciate how annoying some neighbor noise can be.

It follows that some noisy neighbors are unaware they're bothering us, and should not be considered Neighbors From Hell right off the bat. I'll make the point a lot in these pages that noise alone, and boundary violations by themselves, and everything else a neighbor might commit to our dismay, does not mean war. Offenses against our senses are most commonly the result of a neighbor not realizing he or she is causing a problem. Yes, the noise-acculturated are well aware of their violations and will often turn out – after our diplomatic attempts fail – to be Neighbors From Hell. They've often dealt with the likes of us before, and many have been reared on a diet of noise.

This doesn't mean that better neighbors will necessarily take kindly to hearing our complaints. If I don't mean to disturb a neighbor, and that neighbor then becomes hostile or harsh with me about the disturbance, I'm likely to respond in kind.

But even if approached pleasantly by a neighbor, many of us – even the best of neighbors – won't appreciate being criticized.

There is much to be said in favor of putting up with some noise in a neighborhood. Kids at daytime play in their backyard, people walking in shoes on a bare floor upstairs, a dog barking once or twice when people walk by – these things can be very irritating.

However, I find again and again that we take these sounds better – not as an infraction against our senses but rather as innocent sounds being made by neighbors – when we know and like the neighbors. And they can bear much more of us for the same reason. I'm not saying unnecessary nuisance noise that is pervasive and obnoxious should be tolerated. It shouldn't. But I also don't want to be misunderstood about the subject.

No disagreement needs to equal years of turmoil, and no single act of noise is necessarily an act of war.

Lifestyle disparity equals legal challenges in the modern community

When there's a fair degree of consensus in a community toward noise – similar attitudes about what make up the ordinary sounds of life and what constitutes a nuisance – this generally becomes the "community standard" that influences local laws and their enforcement. A community vocal about its distaste for firecracker use, for instance, often gets strict enforcement of substantial laws against it. However, when people with diverse lifestyles and disparate preferences occupy a community or a section within it, it becomes hard to ascertain community standards about noise, and this makes legislating and enforcing neighbor noise laws difficult.

Rare today are the communities with a prevailing homogeneous population, and those are about the only ones able to set community standards that widely reflect the dominant culture. There, when it comes to noise, attitudes among most of the citizenry are apparent and can have more impact. To make the point, here are two simple but rather realistic scenarios:

- In a wealthy suburb, police might quickly shut down a noisy party on a secluded cul-de-sac because those dominating the landscape don't tolerate such disturbance. This is especially so if more than one call is made to complain, if the noise can be heard from a good distance, and the hour is late.
- Police won't aggressively enforce a citywide ordinance against noise, even when loud music is coming out of every other car and house, if that noise is an accepted local custom in a given area. That's because police usually *aren't called with complaints*. If people with cultural and/or lifestyle similarities favoring musical variety at a high volume and bass level dominate the small community within the larger society, it becomes a social norm – a community standard. (I've spoken with members of such communities and many don't enjoy the noise one bit, but choose to tolerate it rather than complain.)

Ah, but lifestyle-diverse neighborhoods are much more prevalent, and they throw the concept of community standards into disarray. Disparate "cultures" (as they pertain to noise preferences) collide, often with none emerging as dominant in number. Softly-played classical music lovers live beside blasting rap fans; some people wake up early and mow the lawn, others stay up late and have friends over until the wee hours.

Lifestyle diversity in a community presents one of the greatest social challenges we face today in our neighborhoods. The thousands of local ordinances now prohibiting nuisance noise at varying decibel levels and times of day suggest the good guys have the advantage. But several factors affect those laws' adequacy, enforceability and sometimes even their perceived legitimacy.

Wider disparities equal higher incidence of conflict. While everyone's interests might get consideration by authorities (the loud constitute part of the public to which police and politicians are answerable, too), none can get complete satisfaction, so some degree of quality of life gets sacrificed on each side, in theory. But in reality, while we better neighbors once ruled the roost and dominated the scene, the noisy tend to triumph in most disagreements over noise.

That's because, in lifestyle-diverse communities, what is considered too much noise is to a large degree *in the ear of the beholder* – tastes and preferences are individualized and resistant to standardization. Who, in a lifestyle-diverse community, should be the arbiter of what is too much noise, noise too late, or undesirable noise? In the following scenarios, who should police side with if disparity turns into a disturbance call?

- There are two apartments in one building. On the top floor is a fashionable young couple who stay up late, have friends over, and walk in hard-heeled shoes over uncarpeted expanses of wooden floors. Downstairs is a quiet couple with a crying baby and a barking dog, all of whom get up early.
- A semi-retired man runs his consulting business out of his home, spending most of his day staring at a computer screen. A party wall away in a neighboring townhouse, a bunch of twenty-somethings signal they've waken after noontime by blasting their tunes, chuckling and shouting, and bouncing a ball against the party wall.
- A suburban renter living between two homeowners lives a quiet existence and enjoys music, which he plays only loud enough that he can hear it. Meanwhile, the kid of a neighboring owner is 14 and has a bass guitar and voice amplification system she cranks up in the side yard only loud enough that *everyone* can hear it. On the other side, unending hammering and power sawing can be heard during an extraordinarily long deck-building project that fills dinner hours

> and sunny weekend afternoons with banging
> and yelling.

Most people will favor those with whom they most identify. If you have a 14-year-old who wants to be in the music business, the last thing you'd suggest is that people like yourself be given yet another thing to worry about like the police showing up. If you have a dog, you know how hard it can be to keep him from barking. If you work at home, you need quiet time during daylight hours when many noise laws are not in effect. If you're in your pre-adulthood years, you realize that nothing matters more than getting laid, except for talking loudly about it the next day. Or maybe you just hold bare wooden floors that lack carpeting in some esteem.

Yet, retirees, children, teens, dogs, yuppies, hipsters and others all live among each other in a lifestyle-diverse community, even in cases where it's made up of one dominant race or other culture.

The name of the game in a setting with people living disparately is forced *compromise*, rather than forced *assimilation*. Police, whose frame of reference and professional circumstances are detailed later, have a lot going on during any given shift, and like little agents of God they just want all the little people to get along. I typically find cops are given little instruction on noise law enforcement anyway – in many areas, officers can't tell you if there even *is* a noise ordinance in town, much less anything about it. So if police involvement accomplishes anything, it's usually limited to bringing some satisfaction to as many parties in dispute as possible; it doesn't much matter if one party is legally culpable and the other is being genuinely victimized when it comes to noise disagreements – typically, if no one has a gun, no one gets charged or arrested, or even fined. If one side wants no noise, and the other wants lots of noise, the compromise becomes *some* noise. The bad guys win because the social issues are too complex for easy solutions and across-the-board benefits. At stake is the quality-of-life for the Good Neighbor Underclass – and it's getting sacrificed pending workable, politically expedient answers that will never come.

Sadly, noise culture can insidiously overtake a community when its standards aren't easily defined. In a low-end trailer park or lower-middle-class apartment building, for example, police called frequently because of multiple noisy neighbor disturbances may actually recommend a complainant consider moving, even though most of the residents are quiet and are complaining about the non-majority. This is not because police afford less protection to people of lesser means, but is the result of police coming to view the noisy as the prevalent citizenry in that setting. Perceived cultural dominance in the wealthy suburb, meanwhile, belongs to people with similar lives and aspirations; a clearer majority seek peace for themselves and safety for their kids. In the trailer park or other non-wealthy environment, prevailing ambitions are *perceived* to be different. Indeed, many good neighbors raising kids live outside wealthy suburbs, but find themselves outnumbered. Therefore, lawmakers and law enforcers see the odds of correcting "the dominant behavior," be it ever so un-neighborly and unlawfully noisy, as slight.

A peace-seeking majority may well exist in a given area, but many within it avoid the deep conflict promised by confronting the situation. They keep their personal standards off police and legislative radar by keeping their own noise levels – that is, *the voicing of their objections to neighbor noise and similar nuisances* – silent. The consequence is the continued spread of nuisance noise from neighbors and other sources. By not addressing, reporting or complaining about it, the numbers of complaints are left thinner

This facilitates neighbor noise's entrée to becoming a community standard in localized areas, accepted by area police and other authorities as the norm. More complaints to police by more people would notify them of a wider dissatisfaction with neighbor noise, and cops and legislators would likely respond positively with better laws and stricter enforcement.

Online Counsel Transcripts
Here are a few samples from the online counsel I've provided via NeighborSolutions.com and from radio call-in programs in which I've participated over the years. Names and some details have been changed to protect good neighbors.

Dear Bob,

My parents have lived in the same home for decades, and a new neighbor beside them is extremely noisy with backyard parties and overnight dog barking. They tried talking to these people, but my parents speak broken English and it apparently didn't go very well. The neighbors called them chinks (they're Chinese) and threatened them. They're very upset and don't know what to do. They don't want to move, but are afraid to leave their house and can no longer enjoy their garden.

from California

Dear California,

Noisy neighbors sometimes don't know they're creating a disturbance, but people confronted about their noise who immediately make threats and use racist language are going to prove to be all-around jerks.

For starters, a police report should be filed for the threat, detailing precisely what was said to your parents (if their English isn't very good, it would be helpful if you went with them to translate). File the police report at the department's headquarters, or call the police to your parents' home if you want the neighbors to see you've contacted authorities. In my experience, going to police HQ is better because it uses fewer police resources, and you're not giving the neighbors a heads-up that they are in some trouble. Make sure the police report includes the basis for their visit to these neighbors – that there is persistent noise – and see if you can file a separate police complaint about that.

Have your parents log all noise and other disturbances, and check in on them regularly to make sure they're okay. Noisy neighbors often have criminal tendencies, and if these people are as ignorant as the facts you present imply, I would suggest your parents could be in some danger and should avoid any contact with these people.

Keep them socially active in safer surroundings – at the home of a family member or local organization they belong to or may be interested in joining.

Should the epithets continue, contact the local or regional chapter of the Chinese Anti-defamation League for advice on handling such harassment. Someone there may be able to refer you and your parents to a victim counseling center, or to a lawyer who can represent them in the filing of federal charges (terroristic threats based on national origin are a federal offense). Keep me informed about how things go and I'll provide whatever counsel I can.

Dear Bob,

My neighbor installed a hot tub about four feet from the property line three years ago, which he runs for 12-18 hours each day! The low-frequency noise is directed right at my family room window and measures 70-80 decibels. I can hear/feel the vibration all through my house and I can't sit in my backyard. I can no longer have my windows open. It interrupts my sleep. Then when I wake up at night, I'm so irritated that I can't go back to sleep.

Initially, I very kindly asked him to do something to quiet down the motor. He told me that I would just have to get used to it. I have become more and more irritated by it the more I dwell on how much the quality of my life has deteriorated due to his selfish attitude. I asked him again and he said I was too noise-sensitive, and he would buy me a bottle of booze so that I could sleep. When another neighbor yelled across the yard to ask him how he was enjoying his hot tub, he yelled back, "I love it, but too bad it wakes (writer's name withheld) up at night." He characterizes me as a curmudgeon and has spoken badly about me to other neighbors. I want to give him a taste of his own medicine – any ideas? Otherwise, I'm planning to file a lawsuit against him.

from Minnesota

Dear Minnesota,

    I generally don't recommend retaliatory tactics against bad neighbors, mainly because the tactics often create a nuisance for other neighbors who we don't want to affect. This is especially so with noise. However, if no one else could possibly be affected, it sometimes works. The problem is that noisy neighbors don't tend to be bothered by our noise, with certain exceptions. One exception deals with lifestyle diversity -- if he were to be making the noise while you're trying to sleep between 11 p.m. and 7 a.m., and he's quiet during 7 a.m. - mid-afternoon, it's a safe bet he sleeps during that time, and you can try to impact his sleep the way he impacts yours, so long as your noise/vibration affects him the same or worse.

    According to Noise-Free America (NoiseFree.org), low-frequency noise and vibration are extremely damaging to human hearing, and agitating to the 30 million people diagnosed as noise-sensitive (I'm not saying that includes you, but if it does, that may work for you). Real estate attorneys and litigators are good at handling neighbor disputes; if your doctor were to diagnose you as noise-sensitive, this would help your case, but even lacking such a diagnosis, rude behavior like this deserves a letter from your lawyer, so long as you're prepared to spend a few thousand dollars to make your point.

Dear Bob,

    My home has been in my family for fifty years. It is in a quiet upper middle class college town occupied primarily by professors and other professional families. In the past two years realtors have been buying some of the homes when they come on the market and have moved in numerous college students as roomers. The area is zoned single family and restricted to three occupants unless it is a family. No rentals or apartments are authorized. This has not seemed to faze the realtors.

Some of my neighbors have resorted to repeated calls to the police to come out and stop loud drunken parties. The culprits just go to court, pay a fine, and continue partying. I am told that there have been retaliations against those whom they think called the police, such as throwing bottles and trash at the homes, cutting power lines, invading their decks and porches in the middle of the night and pounding on the walls. Thankfully I have not yet been the target of these assaults, but lately have noticed one of the male students standing in front of my house with his big dog, taking a "challenging stance" and glaring at my house. I am elderly and this is not a good situation. Now a large group of young women students have been moved into a home just down from me, and have placed a huge sign in the front advertising it as a church! This directly violates the local zoning codes. I did call the City Council about it and the Neighborhood Association but so far no action has been taken, although the police came to investigate and council plans to address it. Cars are now parked on both sides of our street for a full block or more, blocking driveways and traffic. Activity in the house goes on night and day. The neighbors are frantic. Most are older people and they are frightened of what is happening. Between the drunken fraternity boys and the all night cult activities, our quiet life is totally upended!

from Arkansas

Dear Arkansas,

Stay in touch with your councilperson and mobilize your neighbors to appear at the meeting where this will be discussed. Keep a fire under the neighborhood association so its letter is read at the meeting, preferably by someone with the association or the council member you're working with (in a pinch, it's okay if you or a neighbor read it). Show up in numbers because action isn't taken by legislative bodies with any voracity unless there's a groundswell. This is a process, and I recommend taking it all the way if this is important to you.

Retaliation against you and your neighbors can be a serious charge. Snap a photo or get video of anyone glaring up at your home. Your word against theirs isn't good enough in a harassment criminal complaint -- best to have proof. Usually, these complaints are filed with your local court clerk, who schedules a probable cause hearing -- you/your neighbors appear, as complainants, and these guys appear as the subject of the judge's probe. A judge's finding of harassment gives local police greater latitude in making arrests for future violations of any sort – even nuisance noise.

In all cases, consider yourself and your neighbors to be in some danger, because these people seem willing to confront you. They may never do anything, but you shouldn't take chances. Do not communicate with them, and quickly call 911 whenever someone is congregating outside your home. It also helps to obtain reports from police of all complaints when you go to court.

You and your neighbors may also join together to hire a lawyer to represent your interests, to interact with the judge, council and others. If necessary, you can all bring a suit against property owners, regardless of ordinance shortcomings, for allowing damage to your community that has lowered your quality of life.

Chapter 2: Boundaries – The Line in the Sand
Spite fences, cameras, water runoff, easements and shared property

The old "High fences make for good neighbors" saying doesn't cover a fraction of all that can go wrong where *our* little world meets *their* little world.

Boundaries are a state of mind as much as they are a legal dotted line between properties. We all find people who have *boundary issues* in our daily travels.

Have you seen the left-turn driver at an intersection, with three-quarters of his or her car over the yellow line, in the way of oncoming traffic? Dumb drivers make for bad neighbors in a number of provable ways, and the left-turner blocking the other lane is too self-absorbed and dim-witted to understand the concept of any type of boundary – personal or property. They endanger and pretty much enrage the rest of us. I don't need to live beside them to know they'd make for difficult neighbors, who'd see nothing wrong with putting their trash out on collection day in front of my house instead of their own, or parking too far on my side of our shared driveway.

Another type of boundary-ignorant person I come across from time to time is one guilty of premature ingratiation. As described earlier, as soon as you meet this person, you're given too much personal and other information, information you didn't ask for and don't want. Remember Mimi Cass? Premature ingratiation is a sign of not understanding personal boundaries, and plainly stated, boundaries are boundaries. If you think people want to hear your gossip about others or intensely personal facts about your life, you're likely to also think your neighbors won't mind if you build your fence without permits, just over the official property line; you'll give no thought to positioning your pool water drainage hoses where they'll flood a neighbor's yard rather than your own.

To avoid winding up with such miserable neighbors, our best bet is to live neighbor-free, out in the wilderness or at least in a setting where neighbors are far enough away not to impact us. But even if you live in the woods, what do you do when the neighbor several acres away has a kid who builds a tree house on your land, near the boundary between the properties? Distance alone is not a cure-all.

The un-neighborly behaviors and bizarre circumstances that transcend fencing are what we'll cover here. So, let's talk surveillance cameras, easements, shared sewer lines, shared driveways, connected rooftops, smoke, bright lights, neighbors who loiter around their own homes, and neighbors who park their cars in front of our homes.

Like all other forms of bad neighbor, the boundary-challenged are psychotically self-centered, and become indignant when their mistakes are pointed out to them. Boundary issues, which are sometimes resolved through local zoning and building/inspection officials, are mere symptoms of the en-masse movement away from neighborliness that forces us to draw a line in the sand.

Driveway Rage

The shared driveway can be found in urban, suburban and even rural areas, and rarely without conflict over ownership responsibilities and benefits. Think about it – the concrete pavement of your shared driveway is cracked and in need of repair. Your neighbor can't or won't share in the expense, or refuses to allow his side to be altered. What about snow shoveling? What if your neighbor parks on your side because he has too many cars already on his own side? How about one's desire to gate it for security while the other refuses?

The shared driveway is frequently the scene of battle between neighbors who are bothering each other in additional ways (like revving engines, car audio systems, loitering and partying, smelly trash storage, kids at play with their portable basketball and hockey nets, and more).

Denser suburbs are the number-one place to find yourself shot by a neighbor because, when shoveling snow off your side of the driveway shared with a neighbor, some fell onto his freshly-cleared side. That isn't a real statistic, but it happens more than you might expect.

And I'm amazed such stories aren't part of the nightly lineup on the local news, as I drive through such areas and see the ubiquitous 20-foot-wide slabs of concrete straddling a border between two bungalows, the Plymouth Neons of one neighbor parked alongside the Ford pickups of another. Since there's barely enough room to open your car door without dinging the neighbor's car, and since there's a zero-buffer zone where the properties meet, what happens when these neighbors don't like each other?

The answer, often, is years of acrimony, legal wrangling, police calls and all-around misery. If you're considering a new home that has a shared driveway, shop around some more. The shared driveway is the most contentious aspect of suburban boundary problems I come across.

Shared driveways make sense to builders and developers. In many areas, zoning regulations don't prohibit the joinder of property when it comes to driveways, and making a single wide one costs less than making two narrow ones kept a safe distance from each other. Now, I could probably write a whole book on the chummy relationship between public officials and residential developers and real estate folks. Since that's a bit off our topic here, let this suffice: Don't look for town council members to start prohibiting the construction of shared driveways, based on the perils they offer the neighbors sharing them. Every municipal government I've covered as a reporter, or dealt with as a taxpaying resident and business owner, or worked for as a public information officer, contains within those brick walls – built as part of some sweetheart deal – a corrupt culture of contempt for the little people. That's you and me.

The saving grace in the shared driveway dilemma is often the deed, written by space aliens and decipherable only by lawyers, whose galaxy allows them to speak three languages: ours, their own, and that of the aliens. For example, a man who contacted me through the web site in 2006, suffering the trials so promised by sharing one's parking area with a neighbor, related the language within the deeds for the two properties:

```
    Together with the free and unobstructed use,
right, liberty and privilege of entrance and
exit, of a width of five feet, into and from
the garage erected or to be erected on the
within described premises, of one or more
private automobiles used exclusively for
pleasure, but no commercial automobiles or
other vehicles whatsoever, over and along the
driveway as above mentioned and set forth in
common with the owners, tenants and occupiers
of the adjoining premises to the North/South.
```

Is that even a complete sentence? And, does it mean I can only park my convertible out there – the one for pleasure-driving, and not the compact SUV I take to work? Is one's company car a commercial vehicle? Deeds read like Shakespeare plays without the wit. The problem the man was facing was that his neighbors were trying to tell him where he could park his cars – only at the back end of the driveway – so they could pull their inset car out to the road *by driving over his side of the driveway,* so as not to have to start up and move their own car, the one closer to the street, out of the way. His neighbors were obviously so self-absorbed that they saw nothing wrong in expecting the man to oblige.

Aside from having to hire a lawyer to figure out the code, Scott, the man contacting me, was also wondering who's responsible for maintenance and repairs. Luckily, the deed discusses easement:

```
   Until such time hereafter as such a right of
user shall be abolished by the then-owner of
said premises, but not otherwise, and subject
to the payment of one-half of the proper costs,
charges and expenses of keeping driveway in
good order, condition and repair and free from
snow and ice in the winter season so that such
automobiles shall be able to have the use of
passageway, as planned, for a total width of
ten feet.
```

I'm glad we cleared that up.

Now, Scott, who's gay and lives with his partner, relates a story that, like so many Neighbor-From-Hell scenarios, has been worsened beyond the initial concern.

"We never had any problems with the previous owners or with anyone else in the neighborhood the two years we have been here," he writes, "but since they moved in they have parked at least twice on our side of the driveway, blocked access to the driveway on several occasions, and left a note on one of our cars requesting us to move closer to our house so that they wouldn't have to move their front parked cars to get their rear parked cars out of the driveway.

"One night after coming home from dinner one of the neighbors said, 'couple of fags' out her kitchen window and also had two police cars come out apparently to show them copies of both deeds and to make us move our vehicles ... We have never obstructed or even driven on their side of the driveway; if we need to get the car in the back out, we either park the other car out front or move it out until we get the one out from the rear of the driveway.

"We had parked our cars farther back in the driveway but after the last incident where our neighbor actually waited for my partner to come home from work, and then pulled up in her car right next to his so he could not get out, and proceeded to tell him she had every right to access our driveway, and also made the comment that if our house were on fire she would do nothing to help ..."

An argument ensued, and eventually the woman threatened Scott's partner. Both men began fearing for their safety now, all over a driveway. Scott continues in his email to me, "We don't even really care about them driving on our side of the driveway as long as they are respectful, but they haven't been and both my partner and I have leg injuries and we shouldn't have to park far back or any other way on our side of the driveway." Conceding the futility of working things out with the neighbors, he hired a real estate lawyer.

I wrote back:
```
The real estate attorney will be worth the
cost, and will likely give you all the proof
you need; have him or her provide the neighbor
a copy [of the deed] with a brief, terse letter
that puts them in their place.  I would
meanwhile have no contact with this neighbor …
What I like about the "couple of fags" comment
is how it empowers you.  Because she said that,
you can file complaints for harassment … there
are federal, state and in many cases local laws
against such intimidation; on the civil end,
you can retain a civil rights attorney to write
a letter threatening litigation, or you could
just sue for damages already caused … You may
not wish to use being gay to your advantage,
but I say, when dealing with Neighbors From
Hell, use whatever you've got.  [But] if things
haven't become too heated, I recommend
avoidance of civil actions and criminal
complaint reports.  The issue may die down once
the driveway parameters are clarified for these
neighbors.  If not, you have a few items in
your arsenal for the next round.
```

The lawyer determined that neither homeowner is supposed to park in the driveway, that they must keep it clear for either side's cars to travel back and forth between the main road and the garages near the back of the properties (luckily, the garages aren't shared). Neither side likes that conclusion, which I guess means the law worked. The initial disagreement expanded and became potentially dangerous, and now each side is inconvenienced by the outcome.

Friendly neighbors can sometimes work out a difficulty like this, minus legal fees, threats and unpalatable solutions. But much of the time, more so now than in decades past, we don't allow latitude, and it's not being afforded our way either.

Spite Fencing

A spite fence needn't be 10 feet high to send the neighbors a message: We don't like you, we don't want to see you, and want to block your view of us and anything nice on our side of the boundary line. But, the higher and uglier, the more profound the statement.

47

Before this one was built, the spite fence victims enjoyed a distant pastoral view; now they look at a wooden wall.

As with other fencing issues, the spite fence can be combated usually with the support of local zoning ordinances or other community bylaws. These dictate maximum height, setback (how far within the property of the fence owner it must be built, so as not to encroach on neighbors), construction material and method, and more. But not all localities have fencing laws, and some laws don't cover blocked views that result when a fence is built within the confines of law. Then, to put it simply, it's lawyer time.

Easements

The concept of easement is defined by Barron's Real Estate Handbook as the right, privilege or interest that one party has in the land of another. Already, the idea is scary to anyone with a Neighbor From Hell.

Easement *by necessity* is one person's right to cross over another's property for a special necessary purpose, such as accessing one's home or gaining entry to a beachfront or lakefront area. Easement *by prescription* is the continued use of another's property, even unnecessarily, which over an amount of time governed by statute or local ordinance ripens into a permanent right-of-way for the user. Continued use, even without consent by the owner, of our property by a neighbor potentially extends the easement user's rights to the point where he or she might as well be a shared owner.

When I lived in Philadelphia, there was an easement beside my own home where six homes' owners were entitled to use my brick sidewalk, beside my house, to reach their off-street homes. That was an easement by necessity. I owned the land and maintained it, but they got to use it because they otherwise could not get into their homes.

Over the years, some of the rear neighbors had taken liberties on my property – some acceptable and some not. If one wanted to hang around there when talking to another neighbor, I certainly didn't mind. But when one chose to temporarily store building materials there for home renovation projects, I became concerned. Then, later, one chose to begin storing her trash there for the week between the time she wanted it out of her house and the pick-up day. Misuse evolved into abuse once it was evident I was not exercising my ownership rights.

Busy with work and already embroiled in a battle with my neighbors directly behind me over noise, I was hesitant to make much of a fuss about this new boundary issue. Feeling weakened by that battle, I though it would be a good idea to let the new problem play itself out.

I was wrong. These things don't settle themselves, minus an act of God that involves the violent dismemberment of a problem neighbor. Ever notice such acts never strike Neighbors From Hell? You hear on the news about a truck losing a load of sheet metal and it decapitated the drivers behind the truck, but when we look outside and we see these neighbors' cars parked and in one piece, we sadly conclude their owners are safely snuggled in their homes with heads attached.

In time, some back-house homeowners, rallied by my noisy Neighbors From Hell, came to insist my sidewalk was *common property*. One used a ladder to climb my outside wall, adjacent to the easement, to alter the flow of rain gutter drainage at roof level, which ultimately caused the flooding of my basement, home to my state-of-the-art kitchen. Another decided to paint a natural wood plant box on my property a teal-green without asking (luckily I heard her outside and put a stop to it).

Evidence was mounting that I had yet another battle to take on. I assessed what was mine in the area of easement where these people were allowed to continually use and abuse my property. All I had there, really, were the bricks in the walkway, the side wall of my house which was nearly windowless, and the plant box. Oh, yea – let's not forget the old iron gate, bolted directly onto my home's masonry walls, historically (for as many years as I'd owned the place) kept in the open position most of the time. The gate would come to symbolize the simmering hostility regarding my property and its allowable use by my growing numbers of Neighbors From Hell.

It was an agonizing situation, being confronted almost daily by people who were once friendly neighbors of mine, who'd been persuaded to believe my property was theirs, and sucked in by the noisemakers behind me to a war I would ultimately win. They'd slam the gate, which sounded inside my home like the world was ending. They'd throw parties out there, hoping to entice me out for war of words between the have (me) and the have-nots, opening and then crashing shut the gate. A less rational person would have gone out there with a crowbar and spilled some blood; I, however, had already begun writing this book and needed more material. How can I articulate the suffering that comes with such boundary disputes if I haven't experienced it? How can I advise the masses on dealing with such matters, without resorting to violence, if my practice is the opposite?

Like just about everyone, I'm not always as patient as I'd like to be, so I pretend to be for the obvious social benefits. If you exhibit impatience at McDonald's while waiting for your Big Mac, chances are good these days the special sauce will be extra-special. So whenever I've had to deal with any neighbor conflict, the combination of my impatient nature and the anxiety brought on by being involved with conflict close to home, makes my blood boil. And hiding that fact is exhausting, and seems an excellent method for bursting blood vessels in the brain and knotting up the intestines. *But failing to hide it has compromised my righteous position* – I always want to be the guy who remains cool and sees things through to a conclusion I can feel good about. Even if I'm faking it. Still, having learned this the hard way, every calm word I utter when in conflict with some idiot next door probably erodes my stomach lining just a little bit more, and for that I'm bound to pay.

Police, I knew by now, would be of no use in resolving the issue. City officials said they could not enforce my ownership rights, despite the deed's clear inclusion of the property, because over time the neighbors had taken sufficient unauthorized liberties with the easement area to claim it as common land, to which they had rights beyond mere passage. That somewhat closely fits the definition of easement by prescription. Luckily, I knew that before the neighbors did. Nonetheless I had to act fast.

Money and strategic design corrected the ongoing abuse – I made architectural changes to beautify the easement beside my home, while disabling comfortable gathering. Keeping the pathway to its legal-minimum width, I had it torn out and redone with the same bricks, the once solid sidewalk now flanked by sharp-edged evergreen trees. I replaced the gate with one built on an independent post, disconnected from my outside wall. This one, I designed with a lock; I handed out keys to neighbors, further asserting who owned what and who was merely given the privilege of using my property. I kept my design plans and receipts for materials and labor. My next step was to install a surveillance camera pointed downward at the gate and my sidewalk, but that didn't become necessary.

As some of the hostile neighbors moved away (being renters or otherwise transient), others replacing them had fewer questions as to the rightful owner of the easement space. As for those who remained, they came to know their place, not only as it concerned my property, but where they stood in a stable community, in which they'd been able to bond only with transient neighbors and drifters. They were, after all, the original Neighbors From Hell, my inspiration for this book. I was slowly, strategically mastering methods for defeating such people – not because that had been my early ambition in life, but because I'd learned there was no other way to live peacefully in my own home. Good neighbors have to control the spice in the community, or it goes to the Neighbors From Hell.

Not everyone has money to settle boundary disputes, but our ownership rights can still be demonstrated through careful design and involvement in our space. I'd made the mistake of not asserting my ownership early on, which opened the gate (if you will) to the misuse; then I allowed misuse to evolve into abuse. In any situation – whether the neighbors are neighborly or not – we need to watch what's ours, so it doesn't become theirs.

Shared Sewer Lines

I won't get into the analogies inherent to shared sewer lines. You get the point.

My same Philadelphia townhouse offered the challenge of a shared sewer line, which began at a high point in the rear-most townhouse and continued down to the street, after carrying everyone else's household load through my basement, which again was also my kitchen.

Clogs would occur and cause backups. Sweet. Backups would begin at the low end, in my kitchen. I'd have to call a plumber and have the communal drain snaked clear, all because an idiot or two behind me preferred to flush kitty litter and cigarette butts down his toilet.

Then I'd have to get people behind me to chip in for the snaking, and would have to convince my neighbors that they shouldn't flush certain things down their own toilets.

Try telling a neighbor – even a good one – what he can and cannot flush down his own toilet. And when cat litter is labeled "flushable," it's pretty reasonable of neighbors to assume they can flush it and not have to worry about it.

I recall during my renovation that I needed to replace the section of sewer drain running through my house, and what a pain this was.

Aside from the cost and the mess, I had to convince inhabitants outside my home not to use their water for a whole day. Since some already didn't like me, how do you suppose that went? Luckily, most were away that day; they didn't have jobs, so I assume there was a jackass convention being held somewhere.

What I wanted to do was cap the drain right where it entered my kitchen from the rear houses, and simply run my own drain, from my own plumbing fixtures, out to the street. Let the Roaches and everyone behind them deal with the consequences. But I didn't. However, I did have the plumber install mesh so that only those things that should be flushed down would make it into my space.

I could probably have forced everyone behind me to run their own lines under the sidewalk easement, but that would have messed with my plans for the walkway beside my house. Besides, deeded or not, an easement becomes effectively enforceable after its use by others for many years.

Shining Lights

A woman from Connecticut wrote me:

```
    I am experiencing the most absurd intrusion
into my home and property on a nightly basis.
The common floodlight is attached to every home
in our town.  Every neighbor has one unshielded
and of high wattage, and since they are all
newer homes surrounding our 1850's home, they
are directed at our home and property, causing
our home to be lit up like a car dealership.
We've followed all of the "Good Neighbor Laws"
by sharing meals, watching their kids, loaning
them our tractor, fishing a drowned skunk out
of their pool, etc., but the most offensive
neighbors refused to redirect the light
downward, lower the wattage and shield it.  We
politely asked them several times to do
something about it, they responded by calling
law enforcement to make sure they hadn't broken
any law.  The town has regulations against "any
objectionable light" but is reluctant to
enforce it because, everyone has a floodlight!
```

I wrote back:

```
    You're right -- situations like yours have a
negative effect on civilization.  You do have
the benefit, though, of existent law favoring
you.  Enforcement in your community is slack,
as you say, because the community norm dictates
```

```
      everyone has a floodlight.  But I wonder if
      others in your neighborhood have a similar
      problem with lights shining right at them, and
      want it resolved.
         Dealing with patrol officers is difficult in
      such a situation, and I would recommend going
      up the chain to a commander (police Lt., Capt.,
      or other ranking officer in your local
      precinct), to talk him/her into pushing for
      genuine enforcement.  You could, after all (and
      might note this when speaking with police),
      install your own lighting system that would
      retaliate and illuminate all your scared-of-
      the-dark neighbors.
         Sometimes neighbors will shine light on you
      if they have an issue with some type of
      activity happening around your home, in order
      to inhibit that activity.  Usually, this would
      be for a barking dog, outdoor congregation
      that's noisy, or something along those lines.
      Lacking such conditions posed by you, push for
      enforcement.  It sounds to me like you're
      experiencing "objectionable light," and if
      police won't help you as they're supposed to,
      go to your city council representative, who can
      make a call or two to police leaders.
```

I'm irritated non-stop by such emails coming in to my inbox. The people seeking my help don't irritate me – the authorities do. This woman lived as a good neighbor, surrounded by people who were breaking the law and wouldn't listen to reason. That's the injury. Do-nothing officials add the insult.

As my high school history teacher, Mr. Barnes, used to say, when describing his feelings toward people talking while he was teaching, "This really gives me the red ass."

I mean, I've been a consultant to, defender of and apologist for local police for many years. But whether I'm counseling someone with neighbor pet problems, boundary disrespect, physical assault by neighbors, noise or just about anything else, I keep hearing the same thing about the cops. That locale in Connecticut even has a law on the books protecting her from having her home lit up "like a car dealership."

Again, we belong to the Good Neighbor Underclass. When dealing with police inaction, I'll repeat this again and again throughout this book – put up, shut up, or call them on the carpet. When the law's on our side, police are duty-bound to protect us. When the prevalence of neighbors, as far as police and other local officials can see, continually flout laws designed to protect the good neighbors from the bad, they tend to fall back on the notion that they can't alter the flow of society.

Horse manure. Dealing with police inaction in my own neighbor battles – when their action would have solved the problems – roped me into local politics, where I began hob-knobbing with city council members and big business owners, where my low and reasonable voice started to carry weight. I should not have had to go to such lengths, and neither should you. But you might have to.

Police don't always know whether shining a light is against the law. It may be against a zoning ordinance in your town, and police often don't know or enforce those. Check with your local zoning office. Even if there's no law of any type against shining a light into or around your home, it may still constitute harassment, and you can file criminal charges on that basis against the neighbor – to do so, visit your municipal court clerk.

You also have the option of pushing for instituting a law against nuisance illumination, which could take years, or finding a relevant law that would cover what your neighbor is doing. For instance, in Philadelphia, I used health code ordinances specific to risking someone's well-being in order to get local police to crack down on nuisance noise from neighbors and passing cars (like boom cars), citing the hearing damage and stress-related ailments noise can cause. You might be able to state a neighbor's excessive light does the following: 1. disables sleep in your household; 2. draws bugs, including mosquitoes, which could infect your family with West Nile; 3. enables neighbors to use filming equipment in an effort to capture you/others in your household (a stretch of peeping-tom laws, but it could work); 4. constitutes an effort by the neighbor to harass you (this works if there has been a documented ongoing dispute between you and them).

Stay-at-Home Loiterers

If you haven't noticed, I like to make up terminology. The stay-at-home loiterer is an unemployed or under-employed loser whose ambitions don't go much past sitting on his porch, his front steps, in his back yard, in his windows or elsewhere within his corner of the world where he can observe the productive world around him.

What's the harm in that? Let's get a list going here.

```
       1.    Stay-at-home loiterers aren't like stay-
             at-home moms, dads, grandparents or
             guardians.  They're not home for any
```

       purpose. Unoccupied neighbors equal trouble brewing.
2. I call them "loiterers" because their listless presence impacts their surroundings. Their foul language, abundant cigarette smoke, beer guzzling, drug trafficking, and their typically unkempt appearance reduce the quality of life for others, and stand to reduce property values.
3. They're noisy, often playing their indoor music loud enough to be heard where they loiter; otherwise, they set up outdoor sound systems to revel in their own uselessness.
4. A good percentage of NFH victims who contact me describe their neighbors, who offer any number of typical and atypical dispute-worthy problems, as *being around way too much*.

    Productive citizens with daytime jobs don't usually witness the day-in, day-out presence or feel the effects of these people. However, stay-at-home loiterers do affect young parents home with their kids, retirees, and the recent explosion of those of us who work at home quite a bit.

    The pre-adult neighbors I'll describe in Chapter 3 were just the low form of life I'm talking about. They were noisy; they stared down passing neighbors, even those who'd say hello to them; they looked all afternoon as though they'd just waken up, because they had; their front-stoop non-stop cigarette smoking trashed the whole block with cigarette butts, and meant anyone with a nearby window had to close out the smells – offensive even to smokers.

    Those who loiter tend to be lazy. I determined the dirty kids next door would not congregate out front if doing so meant they'd first have to clean dog-do off their steps. Since just about any community has its fair share of jerks who don't clean up big piles of do dropping out their big dogs' butts, I didn't have to go far to find some. I didn't have my own dog at the time, and the one I do have is too small to make a big poop.

    Anyone seeing me carefully lift my find and placing it on the front steps of the house next door would surely say I'm the Neighbor From Hell. But I didn't have to worry about being caught by the loiterers – I did it in the late morning, about the time they'd be approaching REM sleep.

Such a discovery on my front step would irritate me to no end, but I'd clean it off and get on with life. These loiterers, however, upon making the discovery, simply decided to stay in. They chose not to sit on the steps because there was dog-do there. Spoiled and lazy, they wouldn't clean up the mess. They walked around it to leave for smokes and food, taking care to stay away from it. It remained all day, it dried and hardened the next, and was finally washed away the following day. By rain.

It's hard to customize that strategy if your stay-at-home loitering neighbor isn't that nearby, or loiters in his garage, or her balcony above or beneath yours. But the point is this: Upset their activity by adding a repugnant or uncomfortable factor. Set up your sprinkler so it "inadvertently" wets the area they're known to hang out, if that's workable. Order fart bombs, as one member of the NFH message board did with great success. Think outside the box about what might disable the loiterers from their activities.

Smoke and Fires

Maggie from Tucson wrote me:

```
I would like to congratulate you for bringing
this site to the public. It has [helped] me
realize that maybe my problem is not so bad …
We live in a mostly Hispanic neighborhood; we
are both Hispanic. [Our neighbor] has, as I
do, many of the Mexican traditions that our
parents practiced. She cooks flour tortillas
every single day (or at least 5 days a week);
the problem is that she does this outside in
her backyard. She burns wood to prepare the
grill where she cooks the tortillas. My
concern is that the smell of the burned wood
gets into my house every morning. We have
installed double windows, but still the smell
of the burning comes into our home.
```

No, her problem isn't bad at all, comparatively speaking. But it's a valid issue. I wrote back:

```
If this is someone you like, who's otherwise
a good neighbor, reporting her cooking habits
could damage your relationship, even if she
just suspected it was you who turned her in. I
don't know the Tucson code regarding open fire,
but there may be an enforceable code relating
to barbecuing. Is it possible to speak with
the neighbor to try to resolve the problem?
```

```
          Can you think of any solutions that would
          enable her to cook without bothering you?
             A rather passive solution might be to
          establish the area where the smoke most often
          travels from her fire to your window(s), and
          set up a fan near your home that's strong
          enough to blow the smoke away from you, back
          toward her.  Alternatively, if you're
          comfortable talking with the neighbor about the
          problem, you might request she use a fan
          herself, near the fire, to blow exhaust away
          from your direction; however, I don't know if
          this would wind up sending the smoke merely
          toward another neighbor.  Plus, there would be
          natural wind factors that no one can control.
             As you said, there are all kinds of neighbor
          problems, and the worst ones involve hostility.
          If there's no hostility now, do your best to
          keep it that way.
```

It's worth noting that municipal codes typically forbid outdoor fireplaces, fire pits, grills and other fire implements within a certain distance of any structure. Report violators to the fire marshal if they won't be reasonable. Even fires built and operated away from structures and flammable items like trees can be fought by neighbors; if you see or smell smoke in or around your property, call 911. *It's not supposed to be there.*

There's another kind of smoke I hear more complaints about each year: tobacco. Because we're in tighter quarters, renting and buying clustered housing is more popular. And sometimes cigar and cigarette smokers aren't allowed to smoke inside their own homes, so they use their patios, alleys, balconies and other areas just downwind from your living space, be it indoors or out.

Smoke can also travel through party walls and floors, so indoor smokers send offensive odors into their neighbors' homes as well.

Outdoor smoking on balconies is increasingly being forbidden in complex housing, but that's a small comfort to the majority of people whose bylaws and leases allow it.

Clustered housing dwellers can press management about enacting rules when there are none covering smoke. When smoke makes it between walls and floors, those walls and floors are flawed. Unit owners can tear out walls and rebuild them with better insulation. Renters are at a great disadvantage as of the time I write this: Tenants' rights groups deal with landlord conflicts for the most part – I know of no group aiming to help those being smoked out of their apartments by neighbors.

Peeps, Creeps and Surveillance Cameras

I'm finding the surveillance camera to be a potential spite fence for the new millennium. I've seen a steep increase in camera activity among neighbors in dispute, some complaining of being watched by bad neighbors who've installed surveillance equipment teemed on their homes, others who've resorted to installing cameras in and around their own homes to keep bad neighbors in line, or to gather evidence of an array of illegal activities. Police have even been advising complainants to videotape their neighbors so they have evidence in a criminal complaint.

With technology so accessible, using cameras makes sense to anyone concerned about the neighbors. Unfortunately, that goes both ways. I might install cameras in plain view to demonstrate to a bad neighbor he'd best watch his step. But as long as that's legal, he might install his own cameras to watch me in my backyard, or to watch your pre-teen daughter swimming or sunbathing. What's the answer?

People contacting me through the web site, who've installed cameras as a step to correcting a neighbor problem, absolutely love them. They work. Bad guys often refrain from bad acts when they know they're being watched and perhaps taped.

But people who contact me from the other side of the lens have a justifiable gripe. Cameras are ideal tools in the hands of the bad guys, too.

One NFH victim I counseled over the course of months had a neighbor who, among other things, rode a horse nearby while aiming a video camera directly on her, her home and her kids. It was part of an ongoing campaign of harassment and intimidation. And, despite this terrorizing activity, the local sheriff and other authorities did nothing to correct it. She was not breaking a law by riding around videotaping her neighbors.

Even if we surround ourselves with fences and tall trees, surveillance equipment can find us, and this violates our privacy. I don't see an across-the-board answer when it comes to video camera use, since no legislation could pre-determine who the good guy is and who's the Neighbor From Hell. The solution probably doesn't lie within law enforcement, therefore.

Instead, we're left to sort through unique details in each situation. The woman with the horse-riding/videotaping neighbor can charge that neighbor with harassment and perhaps sue. There's no just cause for her privacy to be violated, and she can make the case that such surveillance injures her kids. Or, she can videotape her Neighbor From Hell, videotaping her, and can perhaps have her charged under a peeping law in her locale.

If a good neighbor, meanwhile, is sued for violating a bad one's privacy by teeming cameras on a boundary, the defense would be the bad guy's documented history of unlawful and/or un-neighborly acts.

Fortunately, there are more lawyers in the world than we'll ever need, and some are coming to sub-specialize within real estate law to handle neighbor-specific issues. Unfortunately, not everyone can afford a good lawyer.

Federal, state and local laws are always playing catch-up when it comes to technology, and camera surveillance is new enough where it needs years of study before laws can be written that protect the good guys.

For now, we are allowed – in all municipalities I've studied – to position cameras anywhere *on our property*, pointed outward toward any location, be the target a *public space or a neighbor's private exterior property*. If your local police or other authority orders you to take down a camera you're using to track the misdeeds of your Neighbor From Hell, ask for the law that prohibits your camera use. Or call the ACLU; it's become a leftist organization but still champions individual rights in many cases, and those aren't always the rights of the criminals.

Water Run-off

A Florida man emailed me a couple years ago about his neighbor, who razed an existing house beside his in order to build a new, bigger home on the lot. This isn't unusual in places where property values are high and the housing stock is aging.

This neighbor, though, also raised the land he bought, so that water running off his property could soak and damage the surrounding homes. He didn't have proper permits to do so, but somehow managed to get his home built before any authority stopped him.

Obviously, the man who contacted me, and his other neighbors, didn't act quickly enough. They perhaps weren't paying close enough attention to the construction to see what lay in store. Even if they were, it's not so easy for a construction novice to evaluate what's taking place at a home construction site, in order to conclude there will be problems.

Water run-off from neighbors can be very damaging to our land and structures. Water is any structure's biggest enemy, and soaked low-lying areas draw pests like mosquitoes and even snakes. Even when it's less dramatic than the Florida situation, it's serious.

I keep finding that it's harder for authorities to make a property owner fix the damage once it's done, than it is for a zoning of construction official to slap a Stop-Work order on the builder.

Whenever a neighbor is working on roof drainage, pool drainage, heavy-duty landscaping, re-directing of downspouts, re-pitching of any land, building a deck or patio or driveway, watch closely to make sure he's not making *his* problem into *yours*.

When neighbors know and like each other, there's often no great worry. Calling your municipal zoning and/or construction authority is always an option, to make sure proper permits have been obtained for the work. But when we do know and like the neighbor, we don't want to be reporting him for trying to fix or improve his home.

Permit-pulling is a painful but very valid requirement for most work these days, because municipalities have learned how such work can impact neighbors and the rest of the town. For example, I worked in a town where you were not allowed to drain your pool water into your yard, into your sewer line, or into the street. As that locale's public information officer I researched several tanker companies that offered the drainage service, and they all cost money, of course. But thousands of gallons of chlorinated water running into storm drains in the street, which carry the water to treatment facilities to make drinking water, results in damage to the ecosystem and costs money. Pool and other water run-off is governed for good reason.

Report violations you're able to identify, or simply call your municipal authority when in doubt or you have concerns. They're generally very quick to investigate.

Connected Roofs

The sharing and connecting of property is just a bad idea all around. An older townhouse in a city with party walls and joined roofs often is not governed by a condo association, and each homeowner is responsible only for the quality and integrity of his own roof. If he or his roofing contractor redirects roof water onto his neighbor's roof he can cause thousands of dollars in property damage, but it's hard to prove he redirected the water, or that there was any intent to do harm, or that it was the redirected water that caused a particular damage.

My Philadelphia townhouse roof was connected to neighbors' roofs, and I had the additional issue of my house facing the street, while the six homes behind me did not. Their roofing, air-conditioning and other contractors often wanted to use my roof for access to the roofs of their clients. I was neighborly about it and allowed it at first.

Then I found that having all these supplies and equipment dragged up my façade and across my roof caused too much damage. My gutter was bent and became unfastened from the fascia, later causing a flood inside my home. Oil and tar and paint drops came to litter my sidewalk and the front wall of my house.

Having to put a stop to this sort of thing doesn't make you many friends. But so be it. Facing the street gave me an advantage that others didn't have. I'm community-minded, but I don't believe in socializing non-communal property. No neighbor behind me would have paid for the damage being done to my home, so why should I share with them my advantage, and put myself at such a disadvantage?

A solution for handling situations like this is to make your street-facing home impassable by contractors not authorized to be on your roof. Have barbed wire installed at the roof line, visible from the sidewalk.

The solution when your home is *not* facing the street and you need that access from your street-facing neighbor, is to offer to put money into an escrow account, in order to cover any damage you or your contractor causes. Similarly, only hire a licensed contractor who is pulling proper permits for the work; that contractor is required by law to be insured, and his damage would be covered by such a policy so that your escrow would not be held up for too long (depending on complications in a damage case, of course).

Street parking

If your neighbor's household collects cars, or has more adults living within its walls than tradition once brought, then you just might be plagued by having to look at cars that aren't yours, parked in front of your home.

This is irritating when you don't like the neighbors for other reasons. If you otherwise like the neighbors, you probably don't mind. In the abstract, finding fault with someone's car parked legally on a public street seems petty. But it's a psychological boundary issue.

When my neighbor to the south, or his guest, parks in front of my house, I don't mind. I know and like him. If my neighbor to the north, or her guest, parked in front of my house, I'd be agitated. I don't like her. Petty? I believe so, yes. That wouldn't make it less agitating.

A neighbor whose beaten-up auto is perennially parked in front of your house is a different story – like the neighbor or not, your view is blighted. Or maybe it's an RV or a commercial van or a bus. Local ordinances usually restrict commercial and large vehicle parking in residential communities – check with local police or municipal clerk or manager. Junk-like cars can be harder to get rid of. If its plates are missing or its inspection isn't up to date or you learn it's uninsured, it is not allowed on the street according, typically, to state law.

I find that households with *too many cars* are really households with too many cars that *aren't aesthetically pleasing*. Brand-new BMW's, Mercedes, Jaguars and Range Rovers aren't known to litter public streets; lower-value automobiles receive complaints on the NFH message board more than anything else. More expensive cars are usually garaged or parked safely in the driveway, while the Dodge Shadows and Ford Festivas of the world aren't so prized by their owners that they must keep them in their sights.

Cars come to symbolize their owners when those owners are Neighbors From Hell. It's not aesthetics as much as it is association. NFH victims are found to post on the board their ongoing distaste for makes and models of cars that their bad neighbors drove. It's a form of displaced aggression – more of a symptom of a larger problem than a problem itself.

Online Counsel Transcripts

Here are a few samples from the online counsel I've provided via NeighborSolutions.com and from radio call-in programs in which I've participated over the years. Names and some details have been changed to protect good neighbors.

Dear Bob,

I put up a fence two days ago to stop my neighbors' kids from trespassing, and have videotaped them in the act, amounting to four hours of total evidence (trespassing and harassment).

I was visited by a cop who demanded I give him the tape, and he said he will get a court order to take my videotape, and would state in court that I started all of this.

Their kids are trying to get me to say anything to them so dad and grandpa DEWY and HEWY will harass me more. ALL OF THIS FROM THE HAPPEST PLACE ON EARTH. I am white and I felt safer in downtown Watts when I lived there, than I do in my own HOME OF 45 years.

from California

Dear California,

Police cannot confiscate your evidence. The officer's threat of obtaining any court order or warrant is a bluff, and may even constitute police harassment. I wouldn't be surprised if this officer is somehow connected with your trespassing, harassing neighbors.

Not to diminish the anxiety all this is causing, but if you haven't lived in Watts for 45 years, I must tell you things have changed. Nonetheless, being harassed by neighbors, and then by police, produces extreme anxiety.

Complaints to police about officer misconduct aren't always taken seriously enough, so I'd go straight to the D.A. with your charges.

Meanwhile, keep a tight grasp on your tape, and show it to a police officer of rank (including a roll-call sergeant or higher), during an in-person visit to the station.

If your tape demonstrates trespassing and/or harassment, police should take your complaint and cite your neighbor, who will be ordered to appear in municipal court.

Dear Bob,

I have been living next to the same neighbor for about 8 years, without incident. In fact, we have enjoyed good relations with the neighbors during those years. They have fantastic kids, about half of the clothes my daughter wears are hand-me-downs from these neighbors. I have also received clothes from them for my son. Keep in mind that we have single family homes on very small lots (like 1/8 of an acre). About 3 weeks ago, they started using a new outdoor wood burning fireplace. They had a party going on at their house (a nice quiet party with nice people). However, we were in our basement and didn't realize they started up the fireplace. I had all my windows upstairs opened. Eventually I smelled smoke and went upstairs to find everything very smoky and smelly. At first I thought we must have a fire in the upstairs. Then I realized it was coming from them. I sent my husband over to their house to ask that they stop the fire. We needed clean air to air out our house. At first they said ok. Later it became clear that they kept the fire going. My husband went back and talked to them again. They said "we're not putting out the fire, if you don't like it call the cops." We did not call the cops. About 1/2 hour later they cleared out the party and shut down the fireplace - the whole house got very dark - in preparation for the arrival of the police I suppose. Two weeks later they had another fire. I saw them light up the fireplace so I went upstairs and closed our windows. The next morning I saw them outside and asked them nicely if they could let us know when they were going to use the fireplace so we could close our windows. At first they said "we'll try." About 1/2hour later they came up to my husband and said that it would be "too much trouble to come tell us" and that we are "assholes" and that "if we don't like it we should just move". They also added that they are going to plant huge bushes on our property line. I suppose these bushes will take up a nice chunk of our already small lot. So, although I don't want to call the cops, or the fire dept, or sue these people (our kids are totally friends for goodness sake), we did some research. First, I contacted the Fire Marshall who said that he does not have anything to do with the situation. He said there was some old verbiage regarding nuisance smoke in the county fire code but that it was removed last year. Second, we looked up the regular county code – the code supposedly enforced by the police - same code that covers noise violations - that code [confirmed that our neighbor's outdoor fireplace fits the air pollution definition].

So, we went to visit the local police precinct. They said they cannot enforce this part of the code because they can't measure the amount of pollution coming from the fireplace. They said that if we call them they will probably just suggest "mediation." Third I called MDE (Maryland Dept of the Environment).They said to keep a log of the incidents and sue the neighbors. So what are we supposed to do? Can the police really just ignore the code?

from Maryland

Dear Maryland,

Police fail to enforce codes and laws all the time and have numerous reasons (and excuses) for this failure. Hiring a lawyer will give you less frustration.

I'm more curious, though, as to why these friends have turned on you. Do you have any theory? What would make them start calling you assholes? Are they close or otherwise connected with someone else in the neighborhood with whom you don't have good relations?

Cut off all communication, and don't write any notes to them, as anything you say or write can be used against you socially or legally. Let me know your theory about their change in attitude and whether you plan to go the lawyer route.

I didn't hear back. But with police, fire officials and code enforcers increasingly turning their backs on the Good Neighbor Underclass, we might all be well advised to go to law school. Mark my words: A cottage industry in neighbor dispute action is on the horizon.

Chapter 3: Kids – From Bad Parents Come Bad Neighbors

Today's bad adult neighbors are spawning bad little kids that the kids of good neighbors will be dealing with down the road. And meanwhile, we of the Good Neighbor Underclass have to contend with them.

There's a misperception that if you don't like having kids around, you're an old crank. But it often simply means you've done your child-rearing, or don't plan to have kids, or it's none of the above, and you simply can't stand *bad* kids.

And there are plenty of them everywhere. Back when more adults raised their kids to be respectful, contributors to society, kids in a neighborhood were less a problem. Today, and for several decades now, too many parents have wanted their kids to be their best friends – they want to be seen as "cool" in their kids' eyes, especially when those kids get older and are more likely to get into mischief.

Discipline and punishment have been replaced by video games and too-much-understanding. And not only by parents.

The justice system lets too much go when offenders are under 18. It makes the news when a minor kills someone, and the debate focuses on whether a child or teen should face capital punishment for having committed murder.

When the offense is harassment, however, police officers and judges are found to be very lenient and liberal.

One example is that of an elderly woman who complained to her neighboring family about its cat digging through her flowers and leaving its waste behind. This is not an unreasonable thing to complain to a neighbor about. The adults in that household responded, bizarrely, by giving the cat away. All the woman had requested was that it not be allowed out loose to damage her property.

Although they'd taken this step without it being requested or demanded, the neighbors then took to harassing the woman, as retaliation for having complained. The son, just short of his teen years, would look at the woman and stare her down, *while meowing*. Ah, the innocence of childhood, huh?

Some brat staring you down while making cat sounds can be intimidating to anyone, particularly to a senior citizen. So she called the police and filed harassment charges.

In court, the judge reviewed the case and found the complaint to be lacking in merit. The kid and his parents admitted to the wrongdoing over the course of many months, but the judge directed all parties to try getting along for six months, at which time he would rule on whether the case should be sent to trial.

No plea bargaining, no community service, not even a requirement of an apology to the woman. Judges are uniquely positioned to send a message about respect toward the neighbors, particularly seniors, and this one sent the wrong message.

It's predictable that for the succeeding six months, the kid didn't meow at his neighbor. It's equally predictable that his household will resume its disrespect for this and other neighbors down the road.

Yes, court systems are clogged with rapists and thieves as it is, but I don't believe that's a sufficient reason for letting bad guys get away with harassment. But police, legislators, judges and others continue to be permissive and apologetic when it comes to minors.

No lessons are being learned, except for the one where misbehavior toward neighbors comes with zero consequences.

The Tween

"Tween" is one of those annoying media-generated terms that refers to a kid approaching the teen years. The portion of young life *between* early childhood and adolescence now has a name. What did we do without it?

They used to be called pre-teens, and like any other neighboring human, they can be either a delight or a terror. They're increasingly not being watched by an adult during much of the day, and aren't the beneficiaries of traditional household discipline beyond what Jerry Springer teaches. So they sometimes make for lousy neighbors. They're too young in most cases I've studied to have actual malice in their hearts; typically, their overt acts against neighbors are born of what they hear from their parents, when those parents complain about a neighbor.

When you complain to a parent about his or her kid's behavior, as it impacts your home and community, you may be starting a war that rivals the noise complaint (so you're in double trouble if you're complaining about the little jerk's noise). Parents understandably are defensive of their offspring, and this would be quite honorable if pre-teen children were universally innocent.

Let's face it. Even the best adult neighbors among us today were once pre-teens, and many of us committed un-neighborly acts without true malevolence. Even if you soaped up someone's car windows on Halloween, and even though this pissed off the adult victims, there was not a sufficient understanding in your mind that you could be hurting someone.

Tweens nonetheless wreak enough havoc for the rest of us to be more insistent than we are on the need for adult supervision. Adults can be real jerks as neighbors, as we know, but they're also held to a higher social and legal standard than minors. If your tween eggs my house, police might make him or her clean it up, but if I file a complaint about it and we go to court, it's the parent who sat by while it happened who faces a fine.

That is, unless we get that judge from the meow case.

The Pre-Adult

Jumping ahead in life, a 2003 study by the National Opinion Research Center at the University of Chicago found a missing link between adolescence and early adulthood, and a good look at almost any twenty-something can confirm it.

In the study, young adults were asked what age was appropriate for reaching common milestones like completing school, attaining financial independence, getting married and having kids. Their expectations were found to have shifted in recent years.

People now aim to marry and start a family later in life than in the past. That's probably good for communities, since good neighbors share a common trait of mental maturity, sometimes lacking in young adults.

"Fewer Americans today have achieved these milestones of adulthood than their parents' generation," study author Tom Smith told the *Chicago Tribune*. "On average, they are about a half-decade behind. They are showing less adult behavior, they are not married, they are dating, they are not raising kids and they are out on the singles scene. It's a new kind of maturity."

Sounds to me like a new kind of *immaturity*.

People pushing 25 who live by the dozen in a two-bedroom apartment are not going to make for good neighbors by most calculations. The pre-adult lives off Mommy and Daddy in general, supplementing this income by working in a record shop or café. They vie for later shifts so they can sleep in, and party all night.

I do come across many impressive twenty-somethings. Not only are they doing something constructive with their lives, passing up the hackeysack and beer bongs, but they exhibit strong social behavior. I wish I could say they're in the majority. They're anything but.

Even the best of them, due to being born after 1980, suckled at the teat of MTV, so they tend to be either noise-acculturated or just un-concerned about peace for neighbors.

The worst of them are hideous. It's not only that they're pierced and tattooed beyond ever becoming gainfully employed – it's the attitude.

Self-absorption is an undesirable trait in anyone, particularly a neighbor. But it's dangerous in people given toys and tools they're new to.

I can't back this up scientifically, but I'd bet 90 percent of your area's pre-adults drive like maniacs down your lane, in their improperly-muffled, booming-speaker-enhanced, jazzed up Honda Civics and Scions. Fun-lust eclipses sensibility and adherence to the law.

And especially the local customs among mature neighbors. Like safety, peace and quiet, and being able to ask that an un-neighborly behavior be corrected without having to endure harassment.

What went wrong with these "Damn Kids"?

I see examples of bad parenting resulting in an onslaught of losers entering the mainstream. Years ago I sat at the bar of a local café, across the street from a skateboard shop. Near me sat a disconnected soccer mom complaining about her kid and all his misdeeds. The kid was meanwhile looking at skateboards across the street. Surprised?

He then came over and, while being 16, sounded like an eight-year-old begging for candy at the check-out line, when asking his mother for $75 so he could buy some part of a skateboard he just absolutely needed. Begrudgingly, she forked over the plastic.

Once he left, she told the barista about how "they revert back to early childhood" at this age, and what a drag that is.

Really? "They" all do? Or just your little darling, and others whose parents are similarly unwilling to correct that whiney, childish, selfishness?

Kids like these pepper communities everywhere, and they grow into the Dirty Girl and Huggy Bear characters described earlier. They haven't been told NO enough in their lives, and feel quite unrestricted as they glide through their teens and twenties.

Simply put, bad parenting yields bad neighbors. As kids, the children of over-indulgent but otherwise disinterested parents are a pain to deal with in the community. And as they grow older, they cause more and more harm, coddled by the justice system and supported by the media at almost every turn.

Eventually, most will mate and create little Neighbors From Hell of their own.

No, we who don't like bad kids aren't against all kids or young adults. But we have the vision to see what's on the horizon. And that's why we've coined the expression, "Damn kids."

Helping your own kids, and building kid relationships

It often happens that children become involved with neighbor disputes – those involving their peers and those involving adults. Kids are going to be at odds with each other from time to time – neighborhood bullies need to be dealt with, but there's sufficient helpful material out in the marketplace so I don't need to bog down our prevailing subject matter with the bullying subject.

When your kids are impacted by the *adult neighbor conflict* you're dealing with, it can damage their self-esteem and have other negative effects.

Most important for their well-being, are two points:

```
  • Teach your kids to be good, respectful
    neighbors.  They should learn to say
    hello to adult neighbors, ask permission
    to enter a neighbor's yard to retrieve a
    wayward ball or toy, and to avoid causing
    neighbors problems.
  • Kids impacted by adult conflicts in the
    community need positive outlets to deal
    with the stress.  You may not see it, but
    kids can become highly distressed when an
    adult neighbor isn't nice to them, or
    they witness our conflict and its effects
    on us.  Lots of play and physical
    activity are important for younger kids.
    For pre-teens and teens who are harassed
    by an adult neighbor, I recommend self-
    defense training classes, karate or some
    similar activity to rebuild their self-
    esteem.
```

We as adults must be aware that kids in our neighborhoods are highly impressionable and can be easily affected by how we treat them. Get to know them by name, say hello, smile at them, and buy from their lemonade stands and door-to-door school sales. When a kid does knock on the door to request permission to get his ball, smile and say yes. Consider telling him or her that he can always get it without asking each time.

They're not adult neighbors yet. They don't know the realities of neighbor conflict. Try to keep it that way.

Online Counsel Transcripts
Here are two samples from the online counsel I've provided via NeighborSolutions.com. Names and some details have been changed to protect good neighbors.

Dear Bob,

I have the Neighbor From Hell. It started 3 years ago when our boys didn't get along. Well, I told her a few things like, get your boys and yourself some help and rubbed in her 3 failed marriages, and she has been harassing us ever since.

She started coming out of her house with her video camera standing on her lawn filming us. Then she would snap pictures of us. She would yell over to my children and call them names, then the prank calls started in the middle of night. I finally found out it was her calling from pay phones on her way home from the casino.

She had me arrested. I was passing her boys when they got off the bus and the nasty one (the one that is like her) hit my van as I was passing. I had backed up just to scare him. Well, being the honest person that I am I told the police what I did and they arrested me for felonious assault. We are the victims and I was arrested!! You would think that she had her revenge, but no, she kept it up and it only got worse. I was on probation for 1 year with no restrictions other than to stay away from her. I now had a camera up on my house to get on film just how she was harassing us. The court looked at the tapes that I had and couldn't believe it. They tried to get her to come into court but when she heard that I had tapes she said no. My lawyer also found out that she has done similar things to her ex-husband because their law office handled her divorce.

My driveway lines up to her house. We have basically tried to really ignore this person and it has gotten a lot better, but just the other day I saw the kid (who is not driving) point a toy gun at us and we called the police. This is where it all starts, toy gun and then a real one. We are a little afraid. Why do the nasty ones get away with things and the good ones get caught?

The boy now has his friends harassing us also. We have put our house on the market 2 different times but it is really hard to sell here right now. Plus, I love my house and don't want to move. What advice can you give me? We are not taping anymore because she was taking over our lives and we decided to get her out of our lives by not watching her all the time and we were doing so well and then the toy gun incident happened and we are back to square one. I can't get anyone to listen as they (law and legal counsel) think it's all a nuisance. Please help!!

from Michigan

Dear Michigan,
    Your lawyer should realize this is beyond a nuisance, and could easily file litigation for ongoing harassment against the neighbor.
    Since you have counsel, I recommend you pursue that. Meanwhile, don't give in to temptation as you did by feigning backing up toward the kid, and return to videotaping (passive taping will help -- set up web cameras that catch everything for those times you need evidence). Stay the good guy, build your body of evidence, and sue these people for harassment and all the resultant damage.
    For future reference, avoid saying hostile things to your neighbor when the kids aren't getting along. I'm sure you felt justified in saying it, but it may have helped spawn the last three years of otherwise avoidable conflict.

Dear Bob,
    I currently reside in an apartment complex I like to call Hell. My LATEST neighbor problem revolves around the 20-something kids across the hall, their screaming profanity out their windows- not to mention the ever present noise from 9 p.m. -4 a.m. Last night someone destroyed the Halloween decoration that my son and I placed on our door. The apartment manager does nothing to help. The police are sick of my complaints.
    This is not only having a negative effect on me, my spouse, my 9-year-old (who doesn't understand why people can't be nice), but also my 3-month-old who is waken up regularly by these people.

from Oregon

Dear Oregon,
    Your issue is so typical, I can't tell you. I've endured it myself, and so have many of the people using the message board (your account is validated so feel free to use it any time).
    Police are generally impotent in noise matters, depending on your jurisdiction. In apt. complexes, they tend to want management to work things out. You see how that's going.
    Noise at any hour is unacceptable if it leaves their unit, so management can be called on the carpet. Examine your lease for

terms like "livability" and "safety." I'd set up an escrow account and start paying rent to it as soon as possible, so that management feels a greater sense of urgency, since they're not getting their rent money and cannot evict you because of the escrow. A lawyer's letter wouldn't hurt, threatening litigation against management.

As for the 20-somethings themselves (which I call "pre-adults," using a term from a study of immaturity into the first decade of adulthood), they are guilty of harassment if you have spoken with them about the noise and related issues, or police or management have, and they continue their noise offenses. Additionally, the destruction of your property is a crime itself, and if you can convince a judge it was in retaliation for your police complaints, this too serves as harassment according to many jurisdictional definitions (harassment is generally defined by municipal code or statute). Maybe even more than harassment -- witness intimidation comes to mind.

The message board will likely have more tips, so I encourage you to post your story in detail there. Meanwhile, if you feel the harassment definintion is being met by these neighbors (find your local code online, from police, or from the local library), I would bypass police and file a harassment charge with your municipal court clerk. He/she will schedule a probable cause hearing your neighbors will be ordered to attend to defend themselves. In court, ideally, you'll have legal counsel (these kids will probably get mommy and daddy to hire a lawyer for them so you'll want your own), and at least you'll want plenty of evidence. Get tape recordings (audio and/or video), keep a log of all disturbances and property destruction, get copies of police reports (it usually costs you less than $1 a copy, and can take months for police to produce them -- you may need to file a FOIA request/Sunshine Law/Freedom of Information Act to obtain it), copies of letters to management, and anything else you think could be relevant (if you hire a lawyer, he or she will best advise you along those lines).

Meanwhile, don't associate with these people. Don't write them notes, yet keep your communication with management in writing.

You're not alone. Generally, 20-somethings are transient and subject to infighting, so their cohabitation agreements tend to change inside a year or so. Always, with any bad neighbor, take extra care for the safety of your family and yourself. Neighbors From Hell are generally not bright, make poor decisions, exercise bad judgment, and exhibit an array of criminal traits.

Good Neighbors Rule, eventually.

One final note

As a former reporter, I follow the news, especially as it concerns my pet subject. Rather than attempt to encapsulate one very poignant story from Tucson about bad kids in the neighborhood, I invite you to look this one up on the Internet. Use search terms: Tucson, Neighbors From Hell, and the name of the reporter, Vicki Hart. Her story ran in *Tucson Weekly*, a paper that doesn't seem to exist any longer, but the content is still available on WeeklyWire.com. Here are the first few paragraphs:

```
NOVEMBER 24, 1997:  It's been a neighborhood
under siege. And in the face of the savage
onslaught, cops, prosecutors and courts--for
which Tucsonans, in good faith, pay millions in
taxes every year--seem utterly incapable of
protecting the people who live here.
  Who could be so heinous that the entire
criminal justice system flounders and flaps
like a headless chicken before them? Who has
the power to shred dozens of ordinary, law-
abiding citizens' lives into a tension-filled,
anxiety-ridden hell smoldering over weeks,
months and years?
     Teenagers. Just a few teenagers.
```

Chapter 4: OPP – Other People's Pets

Before I moved to the suburbs, I was counseling suburbanites on dealing with their neighbors' pets – all from the luxury of my city townhouse where no one had a backyard and, as you'd figure, there were considerably fewer neighbor pet issues to be experienced.

My dog Buddy, poking his head up between my legs. I'd found him wandering the streets of Philadelphia in 2004.

I'd grown up in suburban communities and done my diligent research, and I understood that huge numbers of people had issues with barking, pooping, digging, smells and dangers associated with their neighbors' furry friends. But leaving Philadelphia for southern New Jersey exposed me to the more contemporary side of pet-related neighbor disputes. And I found they'd changed since I was a kid. Or at least, what I'd experienced as a kid was not too similar to what people experience today.

The barking, pooping and other issues haven't changed much, but the way people address and respond to the issues has.

Complaining about one's pet often comes with a less-than-friendly tone, the reason being that the dog is left out barking overnight, the cat is digging up neighbors' plant beds to poop, the pet owners are failing to clean up after the animals, and the increased popularity of keeping reputedly dangerous pets.

Meanwhile, on the receiving end of the complaint is someone whose pet is often an extension of himself or herself, according to Phil Arkow, co-founder of the National Animal Control Association. Criticism of the pet equals a *personal attack* on many people, especially when the complaint is raised in a less-than-friendly manner.

Still, Arkow says, "Talk to the neighbor first. Many people are unaware that their pet's barking or pooping is causing an issue for neighbors." Having spent 23 years running animal shelters around the U.S., Arkow says a dog's barking down the street would not even register in his mind, but he knows how disruptive it can be for others.

75

Addressing the issue with aggression toward the neighbor is equally un-neighborly, and promises to stir the negativity that seems to be waiting in the wings in many neighborhood settings. This is increasingly how people are going about addressing neighbor concerns of all sorts, I'm finding, and it doesn't improve the situation – it worsens it.

I personally dealt immediately with the barking dog of Mimi Cass in my New Jersey home, as described earlier, and the dealing continues several years later. That's not because I wasn't diplomatic, but because Mimi Cass is among the group that responds to criticism badly.

While noise is a major factor in neighbor pet disputes, this chapter focuses more widely on pet ownership, the realities of neighborhood living, and the ridiculous maze complainants must navigate to bring justice to pet-owning neighbors who continue their un-neighborly behavior long after it's been brought to their attention in a positive way.

The Maze

And that maze, of course, is not one that you can learn your way through in one town and apply your knowledge elsewhere. Each town, township, borough and county has its own unique ways of handling, mishandling or avoiding complaints and doling out justice when it comes to pet complaints. Many local political leaders don't consider animal issues important enough for there to be any standards and practices on the books at all.

"It's a confusing mess," Arkow says, about who's responsible for what issue from one municipality to another. It may be the police, or zoning, or licensing, or the health department, or any of a dozen other town operations, or a division within one or more departments, that you're supposed to call. And then, responsibilities for policing pets and handling complaints are sometimes shifted from one department to another without notice. In some cases, for-profit animal control agencies are contracted by towns to handle everything from neighbor pet complaints to squirrels caught in attics.

Seldom is the person complaining about his neighbor's pet treated by authorities like a solid citizen who deserves results. Complaints seem to be taken almost personally by some authorities – mainly because they 1) don't want the added work or 2) view such complaints from the people who pay taxes to be served by their local government as "petty."

Arkow, who is also director of "The Link" with the American Humane Association (see AmericanHumane.org) and chairs the Animal Abuse & Family Violence Prevention Project with The Latham Foundation, recommends checking with a municipality's clerk to learn the area's laws and procedures for handling complaints.

Police are typically not very useful in pet problem resolution, unless a vicious dog is chewing off your arm at the given moment you call. In fact, no agency is likely to be particularly helpful, Arkow says, until you use these six magic words: "I Want To File A Complaint."

Agencies and authorities are limited in what they can do to help you without your completing an official complaint procedure. In some cases, this means filling out forms, while in others you need to file what amounts to a harassment case with your local court clerk. In the former, your complaint being documented may or may not warrant an investigation by the appropriate authority, and following-up is left to you, the complaining neighbor, since follow-*through* by the authorities is not reliable across the board.

In the latter, a probable cause hearing is sometimes scheduled, where a municipal judge or arbitrator hears your complaint and your neighbor's defense. He or she then rules on whether the matter should proceed to trial. "Serious" (based on the judge's individual judgment) harassment claims make their way to trial more often than pet complaints unless there are associated harassment aspects. For example, my neighbor's continued allowance of her dog to bark overnight may not constitute harassment in my jurisdiction, in which case I'd be advised by the judge to sue her in civil court. Alternatively, if my neighbor's reaction to my complaint has been to involve her posse of white-trash friends in a campaign aimed at intimidating my household into ceasing our complaints, then that makes for a nice criminal trial.

Evidence is key in any case. Audio and video records, logs of events, photos of off-leash dogs pooping on what is clearly your property, witness testimony that a neighbor's cat clawed your toddler while playing in his own backyard – this is the stuff that separates your case from the many matters of he-said-she-said.

Misplaced aggression toward pets

Arkow says there are those who simply don't like domestic animals. While this is true, I can say as a pet owner who loves his animals like family, I also have no desire to listen to a neighbor's dog bark endlessly. At any hour. And dog-do on my property isn't something I've had to deal with, but it would certainly be a pisser.

I recognize some dogs pose a danger to neighbors, pit bulls and similar breeds being among those with the worst reputations. I know some pit bulls personally and they're great, thanks to having great owners. But those jaws can bite through solid wood, and the mere presence of one in the neighborhood can be unnerving.

Problems caused by cats are very big to those who must endure them, but authorities have little interest in complaints about dead rodents being left in yards, or flowers being dug up. Personally, I dismiss no complaints from those who contact me, but I rank these as minor when not associated with the array of other neighbor issues often attached to them.

Walking my dog recently in the park in Philadelphia where I plan to live soon, I came across a fellow dog owner walking his beagle. He said there were those who lived on the park who didn't like dogs and showed it. He said this soon after Phil Arkow had said something similar to me.

Dogs in parks adjacent to homes are often walked by people who aren't neighbors, but who bring their dogs to what is outside their own community, and some owners allow them to dig holes, bark without being quieted, run loose and poop without it being scooped. Such people aren't our neighbors but cause problems for us as though they are. My future neighbor in the city, walking his beagle, told me of a woman there who occasionally spreads broken glass around trees, for no reason other than to harm visiting dogs.

This would likely be one of those people Arkow refers to. I haven't seen research on this, but I'm not convinced people who victimize other people's pets are simply animal haters.

They're committing a crime, no doubt, and if they'd felt victimized by others' pets, they have now – by turning the tables in this way – *become the aggressors*. They're now the bad guys. The reason I'm unconvinced these people hate animals is because I know the frustration of dealing with a neighbor's pets, and as an animal lover, I find myself getting angry *at the dog* for barking. Logically, I know it's not the dog's fault he's left outside at all hours in all kinds of weather. And when I see him and look into his eyes, all I see is a small dog who could never defend himself against my aggression, if I'd decided to retaliate against my neighbor's idiocy through her dog.

I don't see my idiotic neighbor.

But others do, and I hear horror stories from the owners of pets who commit one offense or another, whose pets have been harmed at the hands of a retaliating neighbor frustrated with the issues and the lack of clear solutions provided by local governments.

Such a lapse in reason is inexcusable, and you won't hear me testifying on behalf of someone whose neighbor's pet negligence drove him to harm the pet. But as I point out in the NFH Syndrome chapter, such lapses can be explained as symptomatic of a broken system, where neighbors are non-empathetic, authorities are impotent, and innocent dogs, cats and other pets are caught in the middle.

Faulty enforcement

Having written Mimi Cass a couple of notes about her dog's barking, after trying to work things out face to face for over a year with no success, I involved the Camden County, New Jersey SPCA. Barking dogs are outside their purview, but I was seeing the neighbor's dog out at all hours in freezing and steamy weather. Once I'd seen the poor guy licking ice that had frozen on its way out of her drainpipe, after hours of barking with no one attending to him, I called.

Two SPCA officers paid her a surprise visit and stayed for nearly an hour, asking questions and examining the dog for signs of abuse. They noted the dog had food and water *inside*, and that it was not left outside at any time *during their visit*. While it's SPCA policy for officers to then follow-up with the complainant, these two did not. Why?

Because of my note to Mimi Cass. In it I complained about the dog noise. As I learned later and have emphasized throughout this book, writing notes to neighbors is a bad idea. I used to accept it as a method of underscoring earlier in-person conversation, but that changed when I found many bad neighbors were using the notes as grounds for filing harassment claims against a neighbor with legitimate complaints. Good intentions in written form can yield bad results; ironically, our attempts at resolving a matter in which we are often the victims of harassment, get used against us in court.

In this case, my note served to support my neighbor's claim that I was filing a false complaint, one based on annoyance rather than any abuse I'd seen. And the investigating officers concurred. So, while I'm not saying you shouldn't donate money to your local SPCA to aid in animal protection, be aware that the SPCA officers aren't likely to pursue complaints when they seem unfounded. Without visible signs of abuse or neglect, officers are left with the word of the pet owner, who's denying any wrongdoing, and the complaining neighbor, who in this case provided the negligent pet owner next door with reasonable doubt.

Attack the problem, not the pet

I would have expected there to be more neighbor pet complaints in urban settings than suburban ones, but Suburbia is the place where backyards are extensions of homes, and often are the venues for so much barking and other problems posed by pets. In addition, Arkow notes, statistics show cities have fewer pets per capita than suburbs.

In any case, I find the suburbs to be ground-zero for all neighbor complaints, with about a quarter of them involving pets.

Addressing complaints about pets in cities can pose greater difficulty for authorities. In some sections of a city, armed police officers are needed to escort animal cruelty investigators tipped off to dog-fighting rings, illegal puppy mills, and all sorts of abuse situations.

In better neighborhoods, clustered housing in a city tends to be managed by an association with rules and bylaws that authorities tend to defer to. For one, it means less work for that municipal entity; for another, many pet issues can and should be worked out within a condo, co-op, gated community or other association of homes.

The problem there is that management is frequently off-site or shows indifference to neighbor disputes of any sort.

As noted earlier, municipal clerks should be able to guide you through the local process of bringing a complaint against your neighbor regarding his or her pet. But whether you live in a high-rise, mobile home community or freestanding home, the availability of community associations should be exploited.

Once in-person dealings with the neighbors fail, the involvement of any given association isn't helping, and the problem persists, it's time to go to municipal court or to hire an attorney to sue for damages associated with the neighbor's pet. These range from property damage and harassment to physical effects and diminished livability of one's home.

Recovery for your abused pet

Abuse of pets by neighbors warrants legal, lawful retaliation, and victims (the pet and pet owner alike) need help in dealing with having been victimized

Arkow says victimized pets need everything from first aid, surgery and medical treatment to behavioral counseling and lots of TLC.

In his work with The Link Arkow draws the connection between abuse of animals with violent crime against humans. Personally I don't see why we need to demonstrate this, since it appears rather obvious, and I'm also displeased that violence toward animals needs this kind of reinforcement. But it seems a necessity in a world that marginalizes pets and good pet owners.

"Unfortunately," he says, "animals are still considered chattel property (like slaves were) and the courts have consistently limited damages in civil cases to replacement value for the animal, rather than for emotional loss and suffering." He notes a case where boys who broke into the Fairfield, Iowa animal shelter and killed several cats was *downgraded to a misdemeanor*, because the collective value of all the cats was below the threshold for felony charges.

But, he points out on a happier note, "Forty-five states have enacted cruelty laws that include some form of felony standards."

The connection between animal cruelty and human violence is an interesting theme – not unlike the link between noisy neighbors and people who are generally criminal-minded. The common denominator tends to be stupidity, but even smart people can be cruel. And noisy.

The commonest denominator seems to be sadism, a trait found in any Neighbor From Hell. And that's why, although I've now experienced just how dreadful a neighbor's pet's noise can be, and I know well enough all the other issues raised by our furry friends, I consider those who'd harm an animal, regardless of what the idiot neighbor is doing, to be the Neighbor From Hell. Our neighbor's pets are actually among the good guys – don't let their owners pit us against each other.

Online Counsel Transcript
Here is a sample from the online counsel I've provided via NeighborSolutions.com. Names and some details have been changed to protect good neighbors.

Dear Bob,
I live across the street from a family with five dogs that are constantly barking, which I can handle, as I have two of my own … I hear "Shut Up!" yelled at the dogs almost 20 times daily. I love

pulling out of my driveway to go to work in the morning and see Dad out front in his shorts, peeing on one of the dogs.

from New Jersey

Dear New Jersey,

You know, SPCA enforcement officials sometimes use their teeth more than police do. Urinating on one's dog is considered abuse. I recommend you start gathering evidence, including video. These people will not become less troubling over time.

Chapter 5: Trash and Smells
The reek shall inherit the neighborhood

Issues of trash, unsightly messes and foul smells seldom stand alone as central disputes between good and bad neighbors. A neighbor whose trash is left out, improperly contained, whose yard is filled with debris, old toilets and auto parts, whose apartment odors stink up the whole complex, is typically also noisy, selfish and potentially dangerous. If not, good neighbors tend to let some minor trash and smell issues go, considering them minor irritants. So long, that is, as they are indeed minor.

Since noise and other un-neighborly forms of selfishness are difficult offenses to fight by good neighbors, and since "potentially dangerous" doesn't cut it for police and other authorities, the Good Neighbor Underclass can use a bad neighbor's environmental violations against him.

This concept is similar to the one Elliott Ness and The Untouchables used to bring down Al Capone: They couldn't nail him on the violence and trafficking of alcohol, so they got him on tax evasion.

Authorities dedicated to fining the messy, the smelly, the zoning violators and their ilk are generally faster to act against the Neighbors From Hell on our behalf than, say, police and landlords are in going after the noisy, trespassing, intimidating jerks that these neighbors generally also are.

Trash invites pests, and today we see growing numbers of people afflicted by "hoarding," meaning they throw away nothing. Rotting food, soiled diapers, deceased pets and trapped rodents – these things become their friends, sort of, and they won't part with them.

As opposed to neighbor noise, when trash and smells affect neighbors we find our friends in the media less sympathetic toward offenders, and less belittling of complainants. In fact, they often champion the good neighbors' cause, but I say cynically, that's only because the stories make for good ink and good television. Dan Geringer reported this story for the *Philadelphia Daily News*:

```
    Port Richmond residents fear new infestation
         THOUSANDS of invading cockroaches turned
    Port Richmond's award-winning 3600 block of
    Sepviva Street, near Venango, into a
    disgusting, disease-prone mess, say the
    furious, frustrated residents.
         During the spring and summer, the tree-lined
    winner of "beautiful block" awards was overrun
```

by hordes of roaches that spawned in the animal and human waste at 3613 Sepviva, neighbors said.

Block captain Miriam Oleckna, who lives next door to the heavily infested property, became tearful when she showed a reporter snapshots of the dog feces, the dirty diapers spilling out of torn garbage bags and the rampaging roaches that might force her to leave the only home she has ever known during her 79-year lifetime.

"I was born in this house and I don't want to move," Oleckna said in a voice on the verge of breaking. "But I can't put up with this. When the judge forced that woman to leave this summer, it was like heaven around here. Then he let her come back."

"That woman's" mouth, Oleckna said, was as filthy as her feces-strewn yard. "Effing-old-lady this; effing-old-lady that," Oleckna said. "I heard more f-words in the two years she's lived here than I had in my whole life. And I couldn't believe the mouths on her children."

"That woman" is Oleckna's next-door neighbor, Marie Bowers, who became equally tearful when she told a reporter how the courts ordered her and her children to vacate their roach-infested home so the city's Department of Licenses & Inspections could fumigate and remove all the roach-riddled furniture. "I felt like I lived in Frankenstein's castle and the people were coming to burn me out," Bowers said. "L&I changed the locks on my front door so I was locked out of my own house."

"Everything they said was majorly exaggerated. Their exterminator said that the roaches were so bad, they felt like a cat running down his back. I didn't have any more roaches than anybody else."

"There was dirt and roaches everywhere in her house," said Frank Fioravanti, owner/operator of Bugs,Inc., who was hired by L&I to fumigate. "Thousands of roaches were very active, especially on the first floor and in the basement."

"Two-and-a-half years ago," Bowers said tearfully, "I moved here from Amber and

> Cambria because my kids didn't know the difference between a gunshot and a firecracker. I wanted to give them a better life. Now, we have nothing. They stripped us of everything I own."
>
> Bowers said that no matter what her neighbors think of her, they won't get rid of her.
>
> "That lady next door is evil," Bowers said, referring to Oleckna. "She and her group think they own the block. Well, you can't pick and choose who lives on your block. I fought long and hard to get where I am. I have the right to live here."

It's a good story about a bad neighbor who believes she's right and everyone else is wrong. Sound familiar?

It's simply easier to get sanitation laws enforced against bad neighbors than it is to get police to handle noise and threats.

This is transferrable to other issues of blight. Bad neighbors who have become so resistant to traditional justice measures are often no match for laws about lawn-mowing, property upkeep, improperly bagged trash, etc. Health code enforcers, licensing and inspection officials, historical commissioners and construction officers don't mess around.

Unsightly messes and un-breathable smells, along with general sanitation and pest abatement problems, call into play much of what can be associated with general bad neighbor behavior. The *Daily News* story continues:

> Bowers' daughter Shannon, 18, who has two children of her own, said, "My mom works. She pays the bills. She's a single mom raising her kids. Those people signed petitions to get us out. What's their problem?"

Notice – there are too many people in the household, some being raised by children themselves. An 18-year-old with two kids? You want her as a neighbor?

> Patrick O'Connor, who has lived on the other side of Bowers' house for 21 years and who says he started having roach problems only after the Bowers arrived, said, "This has been a nightmare from the day Marie Bowers moved in almost three years ago. Her property is full of dog s---, cat s---, human s---, roach s---,

> piles of s--- everywhere. We're all in tight living quarters as it is. This is about people not respecting their boundaries."

O'Connor is right. People who make their problems into *our* problems have boundary issues. As do most Neighbors From Hell.

> O'Connor walked into his spotless remodeled kitchen and picked up a glue trap covered with dead roaches. "I don't have a nest of roaches in here, but I'm getting spillage from her house," he said. "It's sickening."
> Last spring, L&I informed Bowers that "all animal droppings must be removed from exterior property" and that a roach infestation "caused by your failure as an occupant to prevent such infestation" must be exterminated.
> In July, Municipal Judge Robert S. Blasi, who supervises the civil division, ordered Bowers and her family to vacate and "remove all infested items including... furniture, clothing, etc."
> L&I fumigated 3613 Sepviva and four rowhouses on each side, including Oleckna's and O'Connor's.
> Earlier this month, the court allowed Bowers to return home and ordered her to allow future city re-inspections.

Too bad the elderly lady with the meowing brat next door didn't get this judge.

> The neighbors fear that the roaches will return with her.
> L&I will reinspect Bowers' property on Monday and report on Tuesday to Blasi, who will decide whether Bowers is compromising her right to live on the 3600 block of Sepviva by infringing upon her neighbors' rights to do the same.
> "This is all about one family destroying the fabric of life for the other families on the block," state Rep. John Taylor recently told rattled residents. "Unfortunately, there's no home-run ball, no magic wand for dirty, disrespectful neighbors. The courts can fine them, but if you allow bugs to crawl on your kids, what's a fine going to do?"

Come to think of it, if you allow bugs to crawl on your kids, you're probably not going to give a crap what the neighbors think.

> Taylor said the problem was so widespread - "I've got a situation like this about every seven blocks" - that he wants to create "a Dirty, Disrespectful Neighbors Court with real teeth in it. If we want decent folks to stay in this city, we have to do right by them."

Taylor just may be my hero. But can we keep it at "disrespectful," so we can start really going after the noisy and others, dirty or not?

> Oleckna said her first-ever encounter with Bowers was on Easter Sunday 2000, when she returned from vacation to find a handwritten note on her door:
>
> *My Dear Nosey Next Door Neighbor,*
> *I asked you nicely once to stay out of my business. I don't know what your problem is and personally I don't care. I do not bother you and I do not want to be bothered and no matter what you do I am not going anywhere...*
>
> Oleckna went to Easter Mass. When she returned home and knocked on Bowers' door to ask about the note, Oleckna says Bowers screamed, "Get off my effing step and stay out of my effing business."
> That initial greeting, Oleckna said, was followed by two years of f-words, filth and roaches.
> She and her neighbors are going to court on Tuesday to tell the judge they want Bowers out.
> "I've worked hard all my life," Oleckna said. "When my husband was disabled, I worked as a welder, then I packed gaskets to support our family. I buried my husband in February.
> "I love this block. I walk to Pathmark, to church, to my bus. All my friends are here. Why should I have to leave? I want her and her filth and her filthy mouth to leave. I want the judge to know that."

Pet odors and smoke smells were covered earlier, but let me insert a remark from the NFH message board to underscore the point I keep making about how the Good Neighbor Underclass is truly reasonable concerning all issues presented by life in today's neighborhoods, even when the issue stinks …

```
All of my Asian neighbors are excellent
neighbors. I mean, they do some things that
are kind of new to me but don't bother me …
sometimes they cook some stuff that smells
kind of rank. Then again, they might think it
smells rank when I cook ribs.
```

Getting along with our neighbors is important enough to absorb a lot without complaining. But there's a line, and it's different for everyone.

Online Counsel Transcript
Here is a sample from the online counsel I've provided via NeighborSolutions.com. Names and some details have been changed to protect good neighbors.

Dear Bob,
    We live in an upscale development. My neighbor began throwing 5 gallon buckets of produce on her front lawn to "feed the wildlife". This resulted in attracting an entire herd of deer, plus rodents, hawks, buzzards. Then the pet issues started. She decided that she did not need to clean up after her animals. First 2 large dogs, then 3, then 4. My daughter began refusing to use our in-ground pool because the summer odors were so bad.
    She installed a hot tub sound system that I can hear with my windows closed. After the incident I told her she needed to clean up. In a nutshell she told me to go to hell. So I complained to the board of health. She got cited, is now inspected by the BOH and had to go to court for more animals than the legal town limit.
    Since then she has taken me to court for "harassment." She admitted to the judge that she was lying. I have on paper that she lied to the BOH about the dog issue. She has put porn in my mailbox. She flips off my entire family, even my 7 year old daughter when she is out playing. And on Halloween she came on to my property with I believe her adult daughter and slashed a giant inflatable decoration over fourteen times. There were footprints

back to her property and the police did nothing. I have had a new car keyed. Now she has tried to sell for the last 1-1/2 years but could not get a buyer. Now she has sent me a notice from an attorney about an anonymous letter that I wrote calling her an idiot and a wacko. I feel she is now trying to force us to move. Oh, she has been videotaping our property for the last year and a half. She puts statues on the property line of witches, rats, monkey giving the middle finger. She, however, keeps making up complaints. My town court says she can make a complaint as often as she would like. She already has a history of telling lies. Help please! The attorney I saw said there was not much he could do.

- from southern New Jersey

Dear New Jersey,

South Jersey is full of wack-jobs, I'm finding. It sounds like you have a good case for harassment, a property damage claim and a number of matters ideal for civil court. Authorities are often not helpful, but you've received good response from Health.

If one lawyer isn't interested, I'm not surprised -- the right attorney is the one with the fire in the belly, and you'll know when you meet him/her. Don't give up on that path, as litigation is increasingly the way to go in neighbor disputes.

Also, set up cameras just as your neighbor has -- you'll want evidence of all that's being done to you, how she behaves, the condition of her home and grounds, etc.

Please keep me informed.

Chapter 6: NFH Syndrome
Fighting the anxiety

Trying to turn the undeserved anguish and prolonged misery of a Neighbor From Hell situation into something positive, even triumphant, is a bit like trying to turn a snake into a bird. Most times, you're going to wind up with a poisonous bird or a singing serpent, one less appealing than the other. It's the same with bad neighbors.

Dealing with an ongoing war with an enemy – yes, an *enemy* – positioned right beside us, is gut-wrenching. It deserves its own psychological distress category, like Neighbor Rage or Community Anxiety Disorder. I've come to call the stress disorder caused by the harshest neighbor conflict situations "NFH Syndrome." It's not like road rage or having a bad boss or a nasty breakup – it's easier to move on from other negative experiences than it is to get beyond NFH Syndrome.

Before ultimately prevailing against Neighbors From Hell, we may experience great paranoia and self-destructive thoughts. I came to believe my first ones wanted me dead, and I was probably right. Their own untimely passing would not have caused me tears. Wanting bad neighbors to suffer is becoming more and more normal. When our neighbors are hellish, the systems designed to protect us fails us, and we can't afford to battle them with high-tech cameras and lawyers, our innate instinct toward violence can be a 50-cent cab ride away.

Short of going quite that far, inflicting property damage or bringing other harm to a bad neighbor is what victims turn to, and my research shows this is growing.

While it's not condoned, it's understandable. You can have good health, a great job, lots of money, healthy relationships with the important people in your life, and all your ducks lined up in a row, and Neighbors From Hell can infect your mental and physical being like a cancer, changing you for the worse.

Being in a crowded movie theater in front of someone kicking your seat and behind someone who keeps talking still outranks staying home on a night when the Neighbors From Hell are having a party. The harsh outside world, shelter from which traditionally is found in our homes, can become *preferable to our own home* when it's the scene where a hostile conflict drags on – that's the essence of how bad neighbors can destroy the livability of nearby neighbors' homes and change us at our cores.

Lacking positive relations with someone who lives near us – even while the rest of the community can be counted among our friends – is distressful. In a situation that sees a threat of violence – or one that merely involves defiant, trashy creatures who stare us down and speak against us to others – we lose a feeling of safety, of well-being – the traditional benefits of a home and community life.

Some of the outcomes of neighbor-related stress and misery qualify as legacies more than as short-lived results. They include chronic headaches, gastrointestinal problems, sexual dysfunction, panic disorder, heart disease, blood pressure problems, alcoholism and abuse of prescription medication. Painful anxiety makes us abuse our bodies and minds, rendering us foolish enough to believe we can absorb it without long-term consequences.

There were times, during the heat of battle, I felt the world was my enemy, a self-fulfilling notion, as I lacked any kind of useful support and didn't really grasp what I was up against. In severe Neighbor-From-Hell matters, family life goes downhill, work productivity and creativity dry up, and every other aspect of our lives is impacted. Victims of the worst, most aggressive and malicious loud neighbors often feel under siege and beside themselves. In some cases, a hypersensitivity to noise develops, making even the ordinarily tolerable sounds coming from a neighbor unacceptable.

The noisy Neighbor From Hell learns to use noise as a weapon against the people who bother him with complaints. Noise becomes his or her "call of the wild," an announcement that he's on the scene. Other types of bad neighbors find other weapons to use in a similar way. One of the more troubling responses to the repetitious offenses, inside the mind of the victim, is a transformation of personality – going from comfortable to highly agitated, from focused and productive to deranged and dysfunctional – *in a snap*. This reaction can come from merely seeing the Neighbors From Hell or even thinking about them – long into battle, we can become so fatigued that we don't necessarily need to hear or see them to be entirely focused on them. So, choosing to leave home for the evening, or going to work, or taking a week's vacation out of town, provides little reprieve and cannot protect us from previous aggression, hostility and disturbance, because the negativity has become so familiar.

I can remember being at a wedding – my own – and with everything positive that was going on I still had my Neighbors From Hell on my mind. NFH Syndrome is obsession, it's undiluted negativity. It occurs naturally in the Good Neighbor Underclass once we're exposed to today's worst neighbors, and short of moving away, the only cure is *correcting their behavior*.

NFH situations often pit good guys against one another. The police are good guys, but seldom side with good neighbors so become a barrier for the Good Neighbor Underclass to contend with. But I think the most difficult fallout to deal with in a neighbor dispute is *internal*. Many NFH victims have spouses or other significant others who cannot understand our frustration or our continued complaints. They don't get why we become so enraged when the noise or other issues start up, out of nowhere as they often do – why this long-anticipated but still unexpected jolt turns us from happy and productive to angry and obsessed in an instant.

They're innocent bystanders in many ways – they love us but don't understand why we're set off by neighbor issues that continue years after we've attempted to work things out with the jerks. They cannot support us in our battles, making this a lonely one.

One important lesson I've learned, not quickly or easily, is about hatred. In the heat of this lonely battle, it can seem impossible to steer clear of feeling this emotion. *Our hate doesn't hurt the people we're hating.* It is literally a useless emotion, serving no purpose beyond self-destruction, churning in our stomachs. As we mark the half-way point in this journey, let me offer this quote, which took me years to realize, embrace, and stick with:

```
" ... Always remember, others may hate you,
but those who hate you don't win unless you
hate them, and then you destroy yourself."
```

President Richard M. Nixon, August 9, 1974

Online Counsel Transcript
Here is a sample from the online counsel I've provided via NeighborSolutions.com. Names and some details have been changed to protect good neighbors.

Dear Bob,

I am in tears as I write this and I desperately hope that you can help me. Here is the situation:

May 2005, my husband and I were recently married and graduated college. We bought our first home, a townhouse in Pennsylvania. We live between an end-unit and another home. As soon as we moved in, the very loud bass and music of both of our neighbors became unbearable. We were unable to hear ourselves speak, listen to TV, read, etc. My husband and I went to both neighbors, both Mexican families speaking very little English and asked them very nicely to please lower their noise. Nothing. They continue and continue and continued. We tried calling our police department, but they said they can only respond to noise late at night and early in the morning and "even that is difficult because everyone works different hours." Luckily both families moved out and two new ones bought each house.

The first was a thirty-something couple with a new baby. As soon as they moved in they put their big TV on our living room wall. We went over with a bottle of wine and asked them to please consider that our walls are thin and please move their TV or keep it at respectable levels. Well, the first few times they seemed to understand, then they just got sick of it, and refused to do anything. Not one to be deterred, we continued to either knock on the wall or go over there each time the noise became a problem...daily. We even offered to buy a surround sound system so they could have their TV on our shared wall, but have the sound come out at another location...no was their response.

Finally, those neighbors called the police on US and asked if they could make us do something so as not to hear their noise. At that point the police told him to lower his music and told us that we did nothing wrong. Eventually these neighbors, whom we call among ourselves "fat neighbor" has moved his TV, but now he finds new ways to torture us. He dumps coffee and soda on our cars and I have had my car keyed several times. The last time, two weeks ago, I called the police. An officer who had previously come out for car keying said he would talk to this neighbor and then let me know an update. Well, when he went over there I heard fat neighbor calling me names, saying I was crazy, I complain about noise, now I complain about this. Strangely the officer didn't argue with him and never came back to update me or let me know what's going on.

Now flash forward to tonight. On the other side of us is a large, ever growing Mexican family who bought the end unit. They constantly play LOUD LOUD LOUD music. My husband and I knock on the wall and usually that works. Sometimes though we have to go over there and let them know it's WAY too loud. Each time they act confused, claim they don't understand, or just act annoyed. Tonight it happened again. I knocked three times on the wall. What did I get in response? "Fuck you Bitch" So I went over there to ask them to please just lower it. And the Mexicans are on the phone with the police, so I think, good call them. Before the police arrived I tried once again to reason with them, but they just don't get it. They say "it's not loud for me". Well, I said, it's loud in my house, can't you please understand that I can't even hear my TV or my husband, or read a book...I can't even go to sleep with this noise. Then,...the cops show up. They seem happy that we are calmly talking to each other, then the officer that helped with my car walked in and said:

"Lady, you have a real history of banging on walls and complaining about noise. You need to deal with the fact that you can't control everything around here and you cannot bang on the wall or come over and ask your neighbors to be quiet. You must only call the police."

I am confused...I used to call the police, and they told me they couldn't do anything...and I never called the police for noise complaints since then! Now I feel as though the police are turned against us...we make too much work for them about what they consider "stupid stuff." So what am I supposed to do? This cop suggested that maybe my car got keyed because I bang on the wall or ask for noise to be lowered.....is it better to call the cops on our neighbors EVERY time they are loud? I feel as though I am being bullied by the cops and ignored. Our neighbors seem to do whatever they want. I can't take it anymore!

We are not crazy people. My husband and I are college graduates with good jobs and we work hard. With our school loans we can't afford a single family home, so we are stuck here. I don't know what to do. I am on my HOA Board of Directors, but we have no ordinance about noise, and frankly everyone on the board could care less. I was thinking about meeting with the police chief to express my concerns, but they just don't seem to care. My car is being vandalized...ruined....and I can't even seek solace inside my home with this constant bass and music. I can't even call the police because they made it clear tonight that they think I am a crazy neighbor that just complains. Please let me know if you have any ideas for me...we truly are desperate!!!!

from Pennsylvania

Dear Pennsylvania,

You've tried diplomacy to no avail, you've apologetically involved police and they barely help. Believe me, your experience is nothing new in the world of neighbor conflict -- you're not alone. Visit the NFH message board and you'll see what I mean -- tens of thousands of posts, most concerning noise.

[Town name omitted] is a nice enough area, but any town will have police officers and leaders who consider noise complaints to be nuisance calls. In Philadelphia, Mayor Nutter and his new commissioner have developed a 311 line, similar to the one in NYC, to deal with "non-emergency" calls, including those about noisy neighbors. Mostly this is to alleviate the 911 system; the fact is, police deal with some nasty situations and often are at a loss when it comes to any neighbor conflict -- they are not resolution experts. In a way, despite being in good company, you're facing a rather lonely battle.

So here's what to do. Invest in a video device that watches your car 24/7, maybe a computer attachment or camcorder -- whatever. You need proof that your neighbor is vandalizing it; once you have that, file a criminal complaint, offering a COPY of the tape/disc to the police, along with a statement that you've reported past vandalism by this neighbor. Don't expect much to come of this, but take the step. Now, begin logging all disturbances -- the hour, date, who's causing them, general description, and what it's preventing you from doing. Your records should indicate a history of police calls (log officers' names and how they treated you), noise offenses at any hour, and how this ongoing situation has reduced the livability of your home. Get tape recordings, or videotape yourselves attempting to conduct normal lives with the noise. A decibel meter could be used to get a nominal reading of just how loud the volume is and how heavy the bass is, but generally only police or other expert testimony is valid in court for official readings.

File a harassment complaint, maybe two months from now, with your court clerk at the borough hall or courthouse, naming any neighbors you're accusing of harassment; ongoing disturbance after you've repeatedly requested peace and quiet constitutes harassment. Ask the clerk for a copy of the harassment code, which may be local, county or state. The clerk then schedules a probable cause hearing and your neighbor gets hauled before a judge, who will hear you very calmly but strongly present how much this is damaging your life. Win or lose (hopefully you'll win), you could then hire an attorney to sue neighbors who share their noise with you so unreasonably.

On another front, use your clout as HOA board member to get internal bylaws created with stiff penalties against noise and other un-neighborly infractions. Search the internet for neighbor noise content and hand out copies of horror stories, news accounts, and other evidence that this is in fact a problem and you all are charged with ensuring a degree of livability of owners in their homes.

I used to be surrounded by noisy neighbors and it's hell, I know. Noise and other neighbor problems make for a huge social issue that has yet to be looked at on a wide scale. Until it is, stay away from these people, don't write notes (they can constitute your harassment of them), don't speak with them, and yes, call police each and every

time the noise trespasses into your home. If officers mistreat you, complain about them to their sergeants, on up the chain.
   Keep me informed.

Section II.

Corrective Action

Chapter 7: Dealing with the System

Not being criminals, we of the Good Neighbor Underclass usually aren't familiar with the mentality unique to police officers, the internal politics of the police department, or how the system works. Not knowing how to properly interact with the police hurts us when it comes to neighbor complaints.

It's also important to understand the effects of involving the police in our neighbor battles. Calling the cops on a neighbor raises the hostility level. Even our neighbors who look and act like they belong on the "Cops" TV show don't much appreciate it when we call the police on them. We've just let them know that we consider them criminals and, despite the fact that some are indeed committing a crime, most may consider themselves fully law-compliant.

You can generally expect to be talked out of filing a police complaint by officers if they don't see the seriousness of the matter or feel the complaint won't have an impact.

You can also expect low police response priority. Police systems usually don't view un-neighborly offenders as criminals, so the non-emergency nature of the complaint pushes it down to the bottom of the list. In a heavily populated area police response time is so long that a bad neighbor may enjoy his infraction – often noise – through its end by the time officers arrive. Don't blame officers for this – it's a management system problem way beyond their scope of responsibility. Late on a Saturday night can be the busiest time of all for police – that's when the young are out and about, speeding, driving drunk, crashing their cars, getting into fights in bars, etc. It's also when most neighbor noise complaints come in.

Police don't view Neighbors From Hell as criminals. Cops don't often become aggressive in defending the law until an offender is outwardly aggressive in breaking it. In most areas, an offender of any municipal code can be arrested at an officer's discretion, but agreeable, apologetic offenders won't face such fascism. Too much paperwork.

Realize the limited impact police involvement may have. When police do take the matter of a nasty neighbor seriously, the offender often learns how impotent the system designed to protect us is. Involving the police is the right thing to do – much more so than making threats and getting into physical fights – but doing so shows our hand. If the Neighbors From Hell aren't going to sufficiently suffer for their offenses when we involve police, they know how much they can get away with. Insist on ticketing if that is an option officers have.

Even when dealing with repeat offenders, understand that in areas where police are kept busy, the responding officers are usually visiting your neighbor for their first time, since there are so many cops working rotating shifts in different communities. So the bad guy knows all he has to do is appease police. Sorry, officer. In smaller towns, the same officer might come to recognize a repeat offender, but may be sensitive to the damage an arrest record does to his small-town constituents, and doesn't want to write tickets to people he also serves. Take officers' names and cite their visit dates when future calls are made and the arriving officers are new to the case. This shows the current officers you're serious and taking notes, hastening their strict following of the law. It also demonstrates to future responding officers that the neighbors are bad guys, disobeying previous police orders.

Complete a police report or file a complaint for each offense. Indicate the specific law being broken, who's breaking it, where he/she lives, and when the lawbreaking typically occurs according to your trend analysis of the noise log and other violation records. Show your paper trail to officers and offer to provide them with a copy. Your complaint, if about noise, should become part of the roll-call lineup for officers about to begin the shift during which your neighbor will likely violate the noise ordinance. Ensure this is the case by making a call to the local police, and speaking with a roll-call sergeant or other senior officer if possible.

Lack of evidence makes it hard for authorities to discern who's being victimized and who's being unreasonable. As stated earlier, experienced Neighbors From Hell may create a disturbance just long enough to bother us, knowing we'll call the police – it's a talent that belongs on their resume. When police don't witness any disturbance around the home of the address phoned in, and a knock on the door is answered by someone feigning having been waken up, the cops radio back to the dispatcher that the complaint was unfounded as they leave the scene. You can chase the officers and insist your call was founded, but it's your word against theirs when no issue remains evident. Officers say to call them back if the problem returns. Don't look for them to come back on their own.

Build a relationship with local officers and request that the aggressive neighbor is checked up on regularly and cited whenever in violation. Calmly express how damaging the offense is to your life, how you've tried in vain to work things out on your own. Realize they can devote little time to our problem because no one is getting hurt in a way they understand.

Understand the context of cops' lives. Why don't they take most neighbor complaints seriously? Some do much of the time, but after just being on the scene where a cohabitating couple had a fight over drugs, one pulled a gun and the other held up a toddler to shield himself, and the kid got blown away, noise and other common neighbor complaints are not the end of the world to them. Some cops become irritated with calls to shut down parties where no one is being physically hurt, and some even identify with Neighbors From Hell. I've heard of officers even joining in the belittling of the complainant for calling the cops over "a little thing" like loud music or other neighbor issue.

Sufficient use of police as our allies eventually wears down the Neighbors From Hell. Once I found myself in the midst of war with my first Neighbors From Hell, every time I heard their loud music during several consecutive months, I called my local police station and filed a report. This achieved two things. My persistence, patience and appreciation for officers put us on a first-name basis – I became friendly with one officer who made it her business to spend lots of time with the Roaches whenever she was called to deal with them. She'd want to see identification, would ask them if they were using narcotics, and would write up a complete report. The second achievement was that it wore down the Neighbors From Hell. Each time they decided to enjoy blasting their music and disturbing their neighbors, they found it came with a price. Even though tickets weren't written, their time was taken up, and an officer pummeling them with the same accusatory questions became demoralizing. Eventually.

Police officers don't serve you alone. Do not make the mistake of thinking the police are your employees because you pay taxes. Officers represent law and order, not the individual desires of any particular resident, so when speaking with them treat them as the authoritative, respectable helpers they endeavor to be. Focus on the laws that are being broken – not the personality quirks of the Neighbors From Hell. Cops don't wish to be arbiters of neighborly behavior – they simply enforce the law.

I come down rather hard on police systems in this book, and how some officers can more readily identify with the bad neighbors than with we who complain about them. But many, if not most officers genuinely want to help us in resolving the conflict. Always thank officers who respond to your calls.

Also, get political. Angry about the lack of ticketing or other consequences for my Neighbors From Hell, I approached my neighborhood civic association leaders about starting a committee to combat nuisance noise. I needed a position from which I could alter police culture. This gave me access to local lawmakers empowered to beef up noise ordinances and fines, and lent me credibility among local police leaders (who naturally didn't want the head of the area's nuisance noise committee unable to combat his own neighbors' noise due to being underserved). Working with the Philadelphia Police and City Council, my committee convinced the people in charge that nuisance noise was a big problem and that fining offenders would bring revenues into the treasury. That second part got them listening. In my former neighborhood alone, police ticketing of noise offenders (mostly pull-overs of cars blasting their stereos) brings in over $10,000 a month in fines. Cops often then make arrests for other crimes (drugs, alcohol, stolen goods), which they learn about through investigating the noise complaint.

Chapter 8: Prevention

Don't skip this section just because you think you're well past the idea of preventing this problem you've been dealing with. It still contains useful ideas for preventing new problems, and if you ever should move to a new home, it may give you some guidance to better assure a peaceful coexistence between you and your new neighbors.

#1 – LIVE WHERE YOU BELONG

"Where you wake up in the morning is not a trifling matter."
- *Christopher Kimball, Cooks Illustrated Magazine editor*

Most of people I counsel could have avoided their neighbor problems by choosing better when selecting a new home. We all make the mistake – some of us numerous times – of selecting a new home for its kitchen cabinets, manicured lawn, proximity to work or location within a fine school district. It's not that this stuff doesn't matter, but your granite counters and stainless steel appliances won't comfort you one bit when you're waken at 2 a.m. by loud music or chased home each day by a vicious dog or have to spend weekend mornings picking up debris from illegal fireworks or smashed bottles.

When it comes to lifestyles, diversity is overrated. I don't belong in a noisy apartment building, any more than fraternity brothers belong in a gated community or Manhattan co-op. What's good for you is good for your *kind* (people whose lifestyles are similar to your own). Lifestyle diversity is at the heart of most neighbor conflicts I've studied and been immersed in. Avoiding it is difficult and certainly not a guarantee of no neighbor problems, but it builds a good foundation.

Renters: Renters are inherently transient, but some remain in one apartment for decades. Examine your lease for language about livability and safety; incessant noise makes a rental unit unlivable and outwardly aggressive neighbors threaten your safety, and you may want an "out" if things should go wrong. You can generally count on neighbors making some noise, and buildings designed to house inexpensive apartments usually lack insulation between walls and floors. Try to rent where the landlord or management firm requires in its lease that residents behave quietly and respectfully toward one another, or will be subject to eviction. Better complex rentals have active on-site management where crap is not tolerated.

City Buyers: Such clustering of disparate people living diverse lives seems insane. Party walls and floors are almost unavoidable, but our exposure to problems can be minimized: corner- and end-units enjoy a greater buffer zone from noise. Newer construction often provides concrete floors between levels, while older buildings are wood-framed and transmit more noise; carpeted floors, or condos with a requirement for soft floor covering over a major portion of hard floors, reduce noise; old townhouses were not built with fire walls between them, and porous clay brick – pretty as it is when exposed – usually needs to be covered with a well-insulated framed wall to keep neighbor sounds, pests and smells at bay. New or old, clustered housing is seldom built with neighbor issues in mind – developers like profits and well-buffered walls and floors cost money. But as Mike Holmes says on his show, Holmes On Homes, may of us would foot the $5,000 or so to ensure we won't hear our neighbors. Mike lists products for insulation and dry-walling that deaden the sounds of your neighbor's life at HolmesOnHomes.com.

In particular, street noise can be a nuisance in any urban setting, so examine sidewalks for litter, cigarette butts, areas of poor care in landscaping and any evidence of graffiti or other vandalism – all are signs of unsavory crowds gathering or even passing through. Unsavory crowds tend to hoot and holler, loiter, smash bottles, smoke and fight.

Suburban Buyers: A morning show talking head advised viewers to avoid buying a home beside one where there's a backyard trampoline or sports equipment, as these are signs of backyard activity that could impact neighbors. And that's true, but such a neighbor may be appropriate for a family that has active kids, while an elderly couple who may not want to hear children's ball-batting, skateboard-crashing and kiddy-pool splashing should take heed.

The suburbs are ground-zero for neighbor conflict today, especially in middle-class areas. Neighbor noise in the city is somewhat expected and many city agencies are positioned to address it, while suburban police forces are finding themselves grappling anew with the conflicting attitudes described earlier and the enforcement issues to be explored shortly.

Seniors do encounter problems in age-restricted communities, but not nearly as many as in areas where they're surrounded by partying 20-somethings and kids on trampolines. Age-restricted communities are among the quietest.

Any home built on a subdivided lot with no buffer zone other than a fence can be the site of pure hell. One neighbor's issues spawn another's – rodents and roaches mate and spread out, one barking dog calls another to bark, late-night loud parties invite others to steal the idea (and these parties today come with DJ-enhancement or otherwise amplified music).

The big shame in all this is that families tend to need some peace and quiet – growing kids and their exhausted parents need rest. And families dominate suburban communities. It's too bad so many of these families are un-neighborly, and that such a potentially livable area is becoming so unlivable.

Rural Buyers: You're not in the clear, but you stand the best chance of avoiding neighbor conflict by virtue of having fewer neighbors, often further away. But much rural housing is built in clusters, where you'll face the same neighbor problems as suburbanites. Follow the preceding and following tips without regard to your rural choice – nearly a tenth of the complaints I hear of through NeighborsFromHell.com are from people living where you'd think neighbor disturbances could not exist, where sufficient space exists between themselves and the neighbors to avoid such problems. But you'd think wrong. Space alone is not a perfect buffer against hellish neighbors.

General Tips for All Situations: If you consider yourself averse to noise, smells and other infractions from a neighbor, rethink clustered homes like apartments and townhouses, and suburban settings where houses are often built too close for comfort. These are the most ubiquitous housing options for many of us, I realize, so my advice doesn't end there.

Know the overall community. Choose one that tends to be quiet to your liking. Maybe you don't mind the nearby international airport with its take-offs and landings and loud airborne jets, or the sports complex a few blocks away with all the noise it brings, or the adjacent bar district that features overnight revelers loudly searching for their cars outside your bedroom window. But this stuff creates a community norm – an acceptable level of noise that may make it difficult for you to demonstrate a legitimate neighbor noise complaint because your neighbor's noise is lower in its decibel value than the prevailing noise around your home.

Meet potential new neighbors before settlement or signing of a lease. No matter how well suited you and your new community may seem to be, everything rests on the immediate neighbors. These are the people best positioned to make you miserable, and your good instincts will tell you quickly where you'll stand with them. And still, your great new neighbors could move away and be replaced by any in the assortment of jerks, dragging their knuckles across today's neighborhood streets..

Don't hesitate to ask a home's seller, current renter or management group whether there have been neighbor issues surrounding the home you're considering. Not everyone's perfectly honest, of course, but a failure to directly answer, "No, no problems" is a red flag. To investigate on your own, check with the local police. Department policies generally restrict releasing information without your submission of paperwork, but officers who patrol the area are sometimes more up-front about having visited a home frequently due to neighbor complaints. Or, go the paperwork route by submitting the Freedom of Information Act ("Sunshine Law" / "Right-to-Know") request form to obtain police records for the new address you have in mind, and for surrounding addresses. You're generally going to be charged a nominal fee for copies, and municipal solicitors and/or police chiefs are often asked to sign-off on the release of the information, so you can expect some blackened-out area of the reports (usually limited to the phone numbers of people involved).

Nothing beats information straight from the Neighbors From Hell-to-be themselves – visit a prospective new home at varying hours and listen for all the sounds that may make your new home less livable. Visit on Friday and Saturday nights to listen for neighbor parties and unwanted street noise; visit overnight for barking dogs and other environmental sounds that annoy and interrupt sleep; visit weekend mornings to learn who starts up the lawnmower or leaf-blower too early; visit at mid-day when partiers rise and often blast music to relive the previous night's glory. No time is the wrong time to do a little of your own investigating.

Scout the general vicinity for trash, cigarette butts, dog-do, and other things that blight a community. Check the condition of neighboring homes and their grounds; un-mowed lawns and shabby buildings are signs of anti-social behavior.

Take a good look at the cars of neighbors. Tricked-out, pumped up vehicles are noisy and tend to belong to neighbor-haters, and the stupid in general. Auto collections belonging to one household – and I don't mean vintage autos – indicate that perhaps more adults live in that household than you'd like to live beside. As for make and model of neighbors' cars, Range Rover and BMW drivers may find themselves out-of-tune with pickup and subcompact drivers, and vice-versa.

Are the cars parked neatly or haphazardly? Are they parked where they should be, or are they encroaching on your would-be property?

Do neighbors drive up and down the street faster than allowed, or otherwise recklessly? That's a clear sign of disrespect for neighbors.

Examine the lay of the land. Are neighbors' yards at a higher elevation than the one you're considering? Are drainpipes or hoses aimed at your lot? For this and similar issues, have a professional home inspector investigate potential harm coming from surrounding properties.

Do fences, walls and hedges belong to your place or a neighboring place? Make sure about rights and responsibilities before taking the plunge.

Do neighboring homes have a direct line of sight into your home or outside living area? Privacy is important, and being watched by a bad neighbor is not a fun thing.

Look, listen and think. Real estate agents expect buyers to care more about whether a seller has personal photographs on the mantle. Think for yourself. Take it all in and go with your instincts, which hopefully improve as a result of reading this book. Are several homes for sale in the area, particularly surrounding one suspect household? When checking out a rental, do you hear barking dogs inside doors of other apartments?

Know what it is you can and cannot live happily with. Avoid selecting a home with the pie-in-the-sky hope that you won't be bothered by neighbors – do your due diligence and you're better positioned to live NFH-free.

#2 – BE A GOOD NEIGHBOR

It's a safe bet that you already think you're a great neighbor, but many people are unaware of their own faults. Consider this: Neighbors From Hell typically don't consider themselves to be aggressive jerks, but feel they're being victimized by those around them. Are you really that quiet? Are your kids as polite as neighbors might like? Being a good neighbor means having empathy and courtesy. It also means raising your children to be respectful toward neighbors – their friendliness to adults and other kids in the community goes a long way to avoiding problems. A 10-year-old who says hi is more likely to get a pass by neighbors for his loud play than a 10-year-old who fails to politely engage neighboring adults.

#3 – KNOW AND BE KNOWN

Learn to thrive on positive, gossip-free socialization, even if you are naturally shy and prefer to keep to yourself. When people know each other in a neighborhood well enough to smile and say hi, that's sometimes all it takes for the majority of folks to be empathetic and courteous when it comes to noise, boundaries, kids, pets and so forth. Unfortunately, today's communities are often filled with people who *don't want to know* each other; they have friends from work and school and their previous neighborhood and don't care about making more. In this electronic age we rely on the Internet for interpersonal communication and on television for entertainment. We too often don't expend the time or effort to get to know neighbors or let ourselves be known.

When there's unfamiliarity among people living in close proximity, issues can easily become more of a nuisance than when we all know and like each other. My Philadelphia townhouse was surrounded by other homes, and the same music wafting through the wall from the side where I knew and liked the neighbor didn't bother me nearly as much as that coming from people I didn't know or like.

Again, when it comes to neighbors, it's *unfamiliarity* that often breeds contempt.

#4 – BE A GOOD, ACTIVE CITIZEN

Recycle. Neighbors From Hell are selfish, and the more we distance ourselves from their ways the better. What makes us the "good guys" isn't a mere matter of taste – we abide by the laws they break, we're introspective and community-minded while they're self-involved and rude, and we care about the environment while their simple act of breathing pollutes it.

Attend community association meetings, join neighborhood watch groups, know your political representatives and consider running for local office. Buy the stuff your neighbors' kids sell whether it's cookies or lemonade or holiday accessories, even if you don't want it – consider it an investment in neighborhood harmony.

#5 – BE PATIENT

Don't look to me to practice what I preach on this one. I'm learning, and I'm mellowing with age, but patience is not one of my core virtues.

However, jerky people – be they bad neighbors, aggressive drivers or Machiavellian colleagues – generally share the trait of impatience. Impatience is a sign of lower intelligence (but I'm smart enough to hide my lack of patience, and to know I need to hone this skill). Good neighbors of the world indulge a great deal of neighbor nuisances before adopting a zero-tolerance policy against them.

#6 – BUFFER YOURSELF

As cited earlier, we avoid being disturbed by many ordinary sounds of life when we have well-insulated windows in suburbs, and well-insulated walls in the city. A good window will block out the occasional barking or car door slamming, and a good wall helps us avoid hearing domestic quarrels next door.

Use carpeting or rugs to absorb interior sounds. Environmentally, it's best to use area rugs rather than wall-to-wall carpeting, but wall-to-wall floor insulation does the better job of buffering. There are new eco-friendly carpeting solutions coming on the market all the time, make of materials that are recycled and recyclable, and reduce indoor pollution and release low- or no-organic compounds (important for allergy sufferers, babies, the elderly and anyone seeking a healthy life).

Water features like fountains in yards drown out minor noise from surrounding yards; they create a retreat in the bedroom as well, bringing a white noise effect that, when combined with the above, help assure a sound night's sleep. There are many white noise machines available as well, and I hear from people enjoying great results with them.

As allowable by local code, fence yourself in for privacy and avoidance of uninvited guests (neighbors' kids, toys, trash, pets, etc.). Lower fencing is suitable between your home and that of a friendly neighbor; the highest, densest fencing is great for bad neighbors.

Buffering is not fool-proof, meaning that a real fool next door isn't offering what we consider ordinary issues. A rug won't keep you from hearing an upstairs neighbor's basketball dribbling, great insulation can hold back just so many decibels, and the world's greatest fence won't stop a bad neighbor from videotaping your beer gut as you walk across your lawn and then posting it on YouTube.

And when it comes to bass, if it shakes the earth, no neighbor buffer will stop it from shaking your inner ear. But basic buffering methods keep many everyday issues at bay, and employing them means we've done all we can to avoid problems in the first place.

#7 – BE A CONSCIENTIOUS NEIGHBOR

We are all empowered to influence the behavior of those around us to some degree. When we ourselves create issues that leave our boundaries, we're setting a pace neighbors will keep up with. How can you complain about your neighbor's noise if you're making too much yourself? Does your own trash smell? Are your kids behaving well toward other kids in the neighborhood, playing safely and quietly?

#8 – RELAX AND BE REASONABLE

Cooler heads prevail in any trying situation. Reduce your caffeine intake, eat well-balanced meals, get in a good day's physical activity, and you'll be ready to take on adverse situations without losing your cool.

In my research, you'll also find the everyday challenges of community life easier to take. It's a tense world, making some of us ready to take on battles that just aren't worth our time, aggravation and money.

If you have lived beside the same neighbor for 10 years without problems, but last weekend he threw a loud party or made some other objectionable noise, you don't have a Neighbor From Hell. Even great neighbors occasionally exercise misjudgment, and this need not be the start of a war.

Chapter 9: Diplomacy

I'm told by those who know me best and love me anyway that I am not very good at diplomacy. And I admit – the principles of diplomacy conflict with those of a virtue I find more important. Honesty. I guess that's why we hear the adage that patience is a virtue, instead of honesty, and how you catch more bees with honey than vinegar. I'm more of a vinegar kind of guy – I consider myself positive, but I seem to come across to some as sour. That said, I can honestly tell you I do have something to contribute on this front.

More often than not, I'm afraid, telling a neighbor of a problem he's causing is like shedding blood into a shark tank – you've just told someone with a bad attitude toward neighbors how he can bother you more. Most bad neighbors in my research and personal experience know very well they're behaving un-neighborly. But ...

I have a friend from my old neighborhood who was kept up all night by a new neighbor who'd just taken an apartment several homes away, who threw her friends a roof deck party (in the Queen Village section of Philadelphia) for helping her move in. There was happy shouting (drunk people have lousy hearing), blasting music, and the sound of beer bottles smashing against each other with every empty tossed into the recyclables can.

I've had enough noisy neighbors in my time to have a zero-tolerance policy for such shenanigans, and would have immediately called the police to have the party shut down. But he didn't do this. Instead, he and his wife left her a welcome basket the next day, complete with a nice bottle of wine, and a nice note that explained why the party disturbed the surrounding neighbors, requesting it not happen again.

Outrageous! If I lived a million years, I would not have tried this. My friends even provided their unlisted phone number for this new neighbor to call if she needed anything. Well, *the noise never returned*. The new neighbor even telephoned my friends to apologize and to assure them it wouldn't happen again, and thanked them for being such great neighbors.

There I was, supposedly the great expert on neighbor dispute resolution, surprised that so simple a gesture (an undeserved gesture, in my view) worked without a hitch. I'm the first to admit being wrong, and I frankly didn't think such kindness could work with someone who introduced herself with what she should have known was a disturbing party.

I don't think such gestures will work across the board, but that experience underscores the need to give diplomatic efforts a try. It is possible that the offending party isn't aware of his or her

113

disturbances. Apply a neighbor stupidity curve. Be skeptical, but become a world-class diplomat just in case.

Diplomacy is the initial step toward remedying a neighbor problem that's unfixable through the buffering methods, and is workable with a neighbor who somehow doesn't know his or her behavior is a problem for those living nearby. We apply the neighbor stupidity curve, and assume the neighbors are unaware their issue is bothersome to others, or they just figure:

- everyone is up at 3 a.m., enjoys the same crappy music they do, can sleep through their hammering on party walls, and can enjoy reading amidst their yelping splashes in the backyard pool;
- neighbors won't mind if they store their own trash beyond their boundaries;
- no one has ever complained to me before, so everything I do must be A-okay with my neighbors;
- insert your neighbor's asinine assumption here

Some neighbors are guilty primarily of wishful thinking, which overpowers some even after they've been asked to correct an issue. They might think to themselves that we're probably not home at a particular time, or simply that we won't be disturbed if they enjoy their music or other noise extra loud.

Diplomacy requires sincerity, politeness, and an ability to simply communicate an issue without demeaning the other party (so let's keep that *stupidity curve* stuff between us). When trying to diplomatically resolve a difference with someone, we are at a pivotal point between early resolution and long-lived war; therefore, it's best to:

- not treat the issue as though it's annoying and offensive (even though it is), but is simply a "concern" or "something we noticed," and
- empathize with the neighbor to ensure we address him or her as we'd like to be addressed ourselves.

It seems rather unfair that we better neighbors should need to be nice to those who necessitate our visit. But, when addressing a matter that's important to us, best results can come from such diplomacy. At least, better results are more likely to come from kindness than from aggression, most of the time. Diplomacy is not a guarantee of success by any means – as illustrated earlier, it can be seen by some Neighbors From Hell as a weakness. Furthermore, there are some neighbors who are more likely to respond only to aggression, but we should never start out with a hostile stance.

We ourselves would not appreciate being told how we should behave inside or around our homes, and should be mindful of the implications of our request that a neighbor do just this. It's hard to speak in a positive manner with someone who's disturbing us, without coming across as demeaning.

#1 – DESIGN YOUR APPROACH

Different types of disturbances warrant different approaches. Overnight bongo drumming differs from daytime trampoline play. Little old ladies' yappy dogs differ from the skateboarding noise of a 20-something living back with his parents. Design the approach with the receiver in mind.

Adults should bring their grievances only to other adults. Maybe the kids are the troubling ones, but the adults of the offending household are accountable, and going straight to the kids may make them feel threatened and will likely spark resentment and hostility by the parents. Perhaps even a lawsuit or harassment charge.

If your neighbors look and act like criminals, your kind diplomacy could expose you as their next target, not only of future disturbances but of physical retaliation, vandalism and other dangers. Avoid personal dealings with anyone you consider a threat.

#2 – DON'T THINK OF DIPLOMATS AS WEAK

A great diplomat is strong-willed and presents a strong, positive image. It can be hard to balance strong will – the determination to get what you want – with politeness, courtesy, patience, tact and approachability. I know this first-hand.

Don't approach a neighbor with your complaint apologetically. You have nothing to be sorry for. But don't approach him or her aggressively or in numbers (gathering other neighbors to gang up on a problem neighbor is a sign of weakness). You're not there to dominate or intimidate, but to be heard.

#3 – BE REASONABLE AND HONEST

Don't treat the issue as the end of the world, even though it's a royal pain and is disrupting your life. Overstating the effects of a problem, or providing too much detail on its effects, will inform the neighbor you are "a complainer" or are exaggerating even if you're not. You won't be taken seriously with your complaint if you say the problem is worse than it really is.

Don't attempt to be diplomatic when you've just been waken by loud noises from next door – wait until later when you're calmer. When we show impatience with a neighbor, we become condescending, and they're often not quite stupid enough to miss that. I know – they deserve our snippiness, but this will get you nowhere but worse off.

#4 – BE POSITIVE

Prior to approaching any neighbor about noise, make a point of conversing positively about something else. If you don't know someone and introduce yourself with a problem you have, the person on the receiving end may take offense that you only bother to talk to him or her when you have an issue. If you do know the neighbor, it's still good to start the conversation with off-subject, positive stuff.

#4 – BE EMPATHETIC, NOT JUDGMENTAL

Remember above all that most of us don't enjoy criticism and quickly reject anyone telling us how to live within our homes. Avoid appearing judgmental or forceful, which leaves the offender with a sense that you want everyone to be exactly like you, and you cannot otherwise be pleased.

Address neighbors as you'd like to be addressed yourself. Neighbor complaints often come across as personal attacks. Some assurance to the neighbor that this is not a personal attack is often useful. Saying, "It's nothing personal," "I love your dog/kids, but…" or "Take me the right way" are examples of somewhat disarming language.

#5 – DON'T WRITE NOTES

I learned the hard way that our written notes, which followed in-person attempts to resolve a neighbor issue, can be used against us by the bad neighbors and even authorities. Ironically, our notes that *aim to resolve a problem* can be presented by the troublemaker as proof that *we're harassing him or her*. Written words can be taken any number of ways and are more subject to misinterpretation than casual conversation or official police reports.

#6 – AIM FOR QUICK RESOLUTION

I find it exhausting to appear patient with someone who's creating enough of a disturbance to warrant my visit. I've gotten better at faking patience, mindful of its benefits.

Smile: It's disarming and can form a positive foundation that carries through the conversation.

Don't be petty: There is no route between pettiness and greatness. Think of someone you admire and consider how he or she might address such a situation. Personally, I think of Peter Jennings.

Be strong but civil: Use upright posture while remaining comfortable and casual, us a normal voice tone and volume, and don't be apologetic about bringing this stuff up. Slouching and speaking too softly show weakness, while any aggressiveness on our part comes across as lecturing and demeaning.

#7 – SET YOURSELF UP TO BE CREDIBLE

Keep your own home looking good and yourself as presentable as possible when dealing with authorities. Police who show up on the scene of a neighbor dispute are found to compare the homes of those in conflict, noting which is better kept, just as they size up the individuals involved.

A neat home, well-kept yard, and above-average home exterior condition tell police you're an okay citizen. Bad neighbors can have these things, but often are found not to.

To remix my earlier advice, the saying "Familiarity breeds contempt" is not always the case among neighbors – it *can* breed understanding and empathy when things are positive.

Chapter 10: Correction

Most people seeking solutions have found themselves well beyond preventive measures and diplomacy has failed. At this point, your neighbors are using their noise, kids, pets, friends, cars and everything else they can think of as weapons against you. Authorities aren't doing anything about it, and your life is pretty much turned upside-down by the anxiety of living beside a Neighbor From Hell.

Choose your battles wisely. As I said earlier, I've fought and won these wars, which amount to whose culture will prevail – that of traditional-valued neighbors who are respectful of those living nearby, or that of the idiots who seem to have so much in their favor. This conflict takes time, patience, steely nerves and sometimes money.

The money part is particularly biting, because most of the people who contact me for advice don't have piles of it lying around. If they did, they'd simply call their lawyer and have the matter handled. Nothing says "Knock it the hell off" like a lawyer's letter or a big lawsuit. But also, people of great means often don't live so clustered with neighbors, un-buffered from their issues. True, wealthy people do find themselves in protracted conflicts with neighbors, especially where space is tight and expensive, like in New York and other first-rate cities. But having a lawyer means you have someone in your corner, and I'm seeing more good neighbors resort to spending good money to fight bad neighbors.

We live in a broken system, where people aren't getting to know each other and the worst neighbors would sooner see us on fire than correct their un-neighborly ways. Landlords, tenant associations and management groups often need proof of exceptional disturbance before they'll get involved, and have a hard time evicting residents who haven't been convicted of a felony and haven't done material damage to their rented homes. Police enjoy neighbor complaint calls as much as they enjoy domestic dispute cases – when they arrive on the scene they often can't tell who the more guilty party is, and the offense typically disappeared just before they finally arrived.

The war is winnable, but I say choose wisely because this effort may leave you, as it had left me, unable to enjoy your home or community. Prevailing doesn't guarantee happiness. I never used to use the M-word, but I do now say, if your neighbors are engaged in criminal activity, the police and other authorities seem impotent no matter what you do, and the overall community is going downhill, consider moving. Some homes aren't worth fighting for, no matter how nice the kitchen cabinets, the view, or the new bathroom remodel.

But, if you're going to stay and fight...

#1 – FIGHT TO WIN

Attitude is everything. Once you decide to stay and fight, be determined that you will fight until you prevail, that you will sacrifice whatever it takes in order to win, and winning means the neighbors lose.

#2 – FORGET #1

Let's be honest. You want to win, but good neighbors are open to compromise, and are smart about the ways of the world. Our triumph here will not leave us parading down Main Street – all we're going to succeed in doing is bringing the neighbor under control, getting the authorities to work with us, and – hopefully – returning to the once happy home lives we enjoyed before this mess began. Once we've "won," we still have to watch and manage our neighbors' issues to ensure they're kept in check.

#3 – SIMMER THE TENSIONS AND DISARM THE NEIGHBORS

Enemies are seldom satisfied that they've sufficiently harmed each other. Immediately stop any aggressive behavior of your own, and do your best to ignore the neighbor's aggression for about a month (while still documenting everything, as described in point #6 below).

Simmering the tensions gives you control, much the way holding your fire does in military combat. It reduces your own anxiety and gives you a breather in order to assess where you're at and where you want to go from here. It has variable results, but often I find the opponent responds by holding his fire as well, wondering what you're up to.

We helped to arm the neighbors when we voiced our complaints, letting them now they could bother us. Neighbors From Hell are sort of like sadists, and like any good sadists, they need our reaction to the pain they're causing us in order to be satisfied. Holding off on complaining and calling authorities, temporarily, removes from their arsenal that reaction they so desperately seek.

Similarly, follow any period that lacks their infraction with some kind of pleasantness, even in the midst of war. This should not go beyond a friendly nod or smile or hello. I often find that a reprieve from hostility develops into a long-standing ceasefire. It can even be permanent.

#4 – GAIN POLITICAL CLOUT

We must fight the defensive reflex to become hermit-like while in the corrective phase, isolating ourselves from the community and the world outside when we should be out and about, where we can enjoy the sense of community bad neighbors rob from us.

If you didn't already, as part of the Preventive level described earlier, run for a seat on your town council or condo board, or be very active in other neighborhood and civic associations. You need lots of friends when taking on community terrorists, and you want credibility when dealing with all the authorities involved. To make changes in my community in Philadelphia, I joined the neighborhood association and started the quality-of-life committee, which came to comprise dozens of people agitated by, among other things, nuisance neighbors. This role put me face-to-face with local police leaders, who listened to me because I had the clout of a political position, albeit minor.

Your clout also comes with notoriety among not-so-great neighbors, who tend to learn quickly that you're a popular, magnanimous leader who is amassing power in order to topple their aggression. This knowledge often translates into a self-imposed correction on their part. Neighbors From Hell won't take on people bigger than themselves, whether that's in the physical, financial or political sense. In the intellectual sense, they clearly don't mind taking us on.

#5 – LEARN POLICE CULTURE

As someone who counts police officers and leaders among my family and friends, and as someone who's worked closely inside departments, I can tell you that cops don't often intend to put you off when you complain about a neighbor. It's just that they've heard it all before, they frequently work within systems they know fail to do much to curb un-neighborly behavior, and they also – very often – have to deal with hearing our grief because they're not solving our problems for us. Ideally, the police would be a one-stop shop for resolving neighbor differences; the fact is that's not their job.

Police officers don't ticket for noise offenses in most of the cases I've studied and witnessed. Even extreme disturbances often come with no penalty. All the offending party has to do is promise to keep it down, and the cops let it go at that. Should a noisy neighbor become aggressive with the police, ticketing and arrest are strong possibilities. This has more to do with police leadership and enforcement policy than with individual officers' desires to help us.

The police don't work just for us – they're seeking peace, and they'd rather leave with a sense they have achieved a form of peace among warring neighbors, and then be called back when it didn't work. They sometimes want the parties to compromise, even though only one is causing a problem, and this puts those of us in the Good Neighbor Underclass at a great disadvantage. Compromise means we still must endure some issue from the trouble-causing neighbor. That counts in the NFH win column, but we should still express understanding and acceptance with officers who are making the effort, even though we know it won't last. Telling an officer his work won't have the desired effect is off-putting – our compliance as good neighbors builds mutual respect, which is important because *bad neighbors seem often to know how to bond with the cops.* Cops like leaving the scene having bonded – they remember those with whom they bonded as the good guys. Bond.

Police officers are highly skilled professionals when dealing with hard criminals who are armed or otherwise dangerous. When we call them about an unarmed neighbor, many find this beneath their qualifications. They sometimes feel there are a lot worse things they need to be ensuring aren't happening, while they're stuck taking a report about what a jerk your neighbor is. The fact is, resolving neighbor differences is simply beyond their qualifications in just about every case I know of. Neighbor dispute resolution requires a great deal of time and expertise, consideration of all sides, and the ultimate prevailing (if I'm handling the matter) of the good, quiet neighbor. Cops don't have that kind of time, and don't like for one side to win because they often don't see the un-neighborly as the bad guys. Police officers frequently are unaware of their own local noise laws, and even if they are, don't rate our noisy neighbors on the criminal food chain beside violent attackers, drunk drivers, murderers and rapists.

In large police districts, responding officers may be arriving on the scene individually for the first time – no matter how many times you've called the police before. So they don't know the history of your neighbor's antics. Police rotate shifts and locations in larger departments, so we often can't make a connection with one officer who'll be with us going forward. So …

- keep a log of incidents, obtain ing copies of all police reports
- note the names of all officers who've visited you
- present as much physical evidence as possible when they arrive

Disturbance complaints are given greater credibility when they're taped – a good audio or video recording of what you called about is useful when the antics stop just after the police arrive on the scene. When the cops don't witness the infraction, they sometimes don't even talk to the caller or knock on the offender's door – they leave and radio back to the dispatcher that the complaint is unfounded. Then, the next time you call, you have beside your name and number the flagging that you've called before about nothing, slowing police response time and even eliminating response all together in some districts.

Remember that the moment an officer arrives, he or she begins sizing up the players to get a vibe. The bad guys to them are inconsistent (dishonest) and interrupting (disrespectful) – be clear, calm and don't exaggerate the facts.

Start considering police to be case builders rather than problem solvers. Their reports enjoy the greatest credibility in municipal court, where you may find yourself next.

Great idea, but ...

There are two key changes needed, in order to elevate the Good Neighbor Underclass into a protected class of citizens, or at least back up to where we used to be:

First, police need to write tickets for un-neighborly behavior, even if it appears no specific law is being broken, in order for municipal judges to become involved with neighbor dispute situations without additional legwork by NFH victims. The system has heretofore rejected the notion, due to clogged, inefficiently run courts.

Second, police need to be more connected than they are to other authorities, and to each other. If your neighbor is violating a fire code by burning leaves beside your bedroom window, and you don't want to call the fire department, calling the police should equal further-reaching results than it does. Police may come out, order him to stop and take a report of your complaint. But the fire marshal should be informed of the violation and often is not. The same goes for zoning violations – zoning officials don't work overnight, so police are sometimes called when someone's building an illegal fence without a permit or violating some other zoning/building code after business hours. That official should, as a matter of procedure, be dispatched the next working day to the scene of the call. I say as someone who's worked within municipal government and directly with police that this is completely achievable.

#6 – KEEP EXCELLENT RECORDS

Log all incidents, noting date, time, duration of disturbance, its nature, if and when you called police or other authorities and if and when they showed up, names of people involved (neighbors, visitors – all by name whenever known to you), names of officers who respond, the outcome of the call, and a reference to your evidence if you have any. In many cases, a small digital tape recorder (under $50) is useful, and it enumerates recordings; note the number on your log that corresponds to your taping.

Obtain police reports you've filed, and those filed falsely against you by neighbors. As noted earlier, you may need to submit a Freedom of Information Act request form to obtain such reports, and may have to pay for any copies the police provide. Consider it a good investment.

Note in your logs or other records how these disturbances have affected your household. For example, did you lose sleep? How much will your property damage cost? Were you unable to complete a project the next day due to having to handle un-neighborly neighbor situations? Were your kids impacted? Did the situation interfere with sexual activity between spouses or cause a fight within the household? Any effect at all should be documented for later.

#7 – STOP BEING A GREAT NEIGHBOR TO YOUR BAD NEIGHBORS

Kindness is weakness to bona-fide Neighbors From Hell. Enough bad neighbors refuse to comply with reasonable wishes for peace that I've experimented with giving them a taste of their own medicine. This is not ideal – I don't like to sink to their level, and there's a strong risk of disturbing other, better neighbors. But under the right circumstances, this method lets the noisy know – while they aren't ticketed or otherwise penalized – that there is indeed a penalty to be paid for disturbing our peace.

When I lived in the city, one set of noisy, trashy kids living in the small townhouse beside mine would simply not stop their loud, all-night partying. Police were impotent. And as we all know well, noisy neighbors love to retaliate against those who complain. So their noise just continued.

But because we of the Good Neighbor Underclass aren't built for conflict, it often escapes us that we are equally well positioned to disturb them, as they are to disturb us. I generally rise and turn in with the rest of the world, so overnight parties just won't stand. Since they continued unabated, after diplomacy and police calls, I took on a renovation project centered on the party wall, beginning daily at 7 a.m. I could have started at noon and still waken the idiots, but 7 a.m. was the legally allowable time to do such work.

Partiers can sleep through an awful lot of noise after they pass out, so our noise has to be impressive. I forewarned my better neighbors of the project and the real reason behind it, and got their support. The party wall became the target of every imaginable vibrating piece of equipment, hammer and nail. And it achieved the desired effect – I successfully put the kids *on my sleep schedule*, and repeated my method each time there was any overnight disturbance. Overnight disturbances eventually stopped.

Later, as noted before, Mimi Cass' barking dog was left outside late at night and even overnight, well after my wife and I politely asked her – after having enjoyed many months of positive interaction after we moved in beside her – to mind the noise. She would not. In us she had great neighbors, quiet people who gave her respect and let her sleep well past normal wake-up time. In fact, after we asked her nicely, she retaliated by having her kids egg our house and scream late into the summer nights on their trampoline, placed strategically beneath our bedroom window.

What she was forgetting, aside from the Golden Rule about being neighborly and doing unto others, etc., is that her home's bedrooms are positioned beside our driveway, where our car alarms going off at 5 a.m., intermittently and for varying durations, would limit the sleep she and her kids might get after turning in three hours before. But she learned. It took doing it several times (noisy Neighbors From Hell aren't always so quick to get the point), and she still requires a reminder course in the consequences of making late-night noise, but it seldom happens now. When it does, the alarm key is kept in our nightstands.

In all this, it's important to remember that noisy people, with their associated criminal tendencies, should be considered dangerous. Remember from Chapter 1 that in 2006, a woman in New York complained to a man working in a neighboring apartment about his noise, and he followed her back to her home and bludgeoned her with his tools. While this may not happen every day, it can and it does. Fighting criminals is for police – not the

Good Neighbor Underclass. Never approach someone your instincts tell you is unapproachable.

#8 – DON'T OVER-INVOLVE YOUR BETTER NEIGHBORS

Better neighbors don't want to be immersed in our conflicts, and can't be counted on for support in most cases I've studied, even if they're our close friends. Teaming up against a neighbor is the stuff of the bad guys – they involve others who readily become part of the conflict because, like our Neighbors From Hell, they are idiots. Why else would they be associated with our stupid neighbors?

Our good neighbors, like ourselves, are positive people, not seeking a fight. Confiding in friends to a limited degree is understandable and I've done this, but be careful not to overdo it. Better neighbors may come to view us as exceedingly negative and whiney when we fall into a cycle of being victims, focused too intently on the jerks next door. Don't make the mistake of further isolating yourself by pushing away the better neighbors. Share an issue if you'd like, but leave it at that. Accept the fact that you're going this alone.

Similarly, do not become engaged in the battles of others. You can offer moral support, but anyone who becomes involved in someone else's war is still liable for damage – even damage done to a bad neighbor. Teaming up with a friend who thinks his is a Neighbor From Hell, exposes you to a harassment complaint brought by the person you teamed up against. And, whether that person was right or wrong to begin with, your decision to join the fight against him rightly makes you potentially culpable in a harassment charge and/or lawsuit.

#9 – ENGAGE THE LEGAL SYSTEM

Know the local ordinances and codes concerning noise, unleashed pets, kids' streetside basketball hoops, fencing, swimming pools, etc. Ascertain they're being broken, and develop evidence against the trouble-making neighbors. Ordinance copies are available from police departments, town council offices and municipal libraries.

Having great logs, a file folder full of police reports, and a reasonably good relationship with all the officers who've responded to your complaints, persistent problems coming from a neighbor now deserve a harassment complaint.

These typically aren't being handled by police departments any longer, but give it a shot. You'll likely be referred to your local court clerk, with whom you can file the complaint, and he or she will schedule a probable cause hearing where you'll present your case and your neighbors will have to defend themselves. Whatever your local justice system employs, use it now.

It's a good idea to have a lawyer present your case, and good lawyers are worth the investment at this stage – the neighbors aren't budging, you're not moving away, the local authorities aren't helping, and perhaps even your own retaliatory measures aren't putting a dent in their ways. You may need to sue them for monetary and other damages, so engaging counsel during the criminal harassment case helps set the foundation.

Many readers don't have this option. That's why you kept the great records and built a rapport with local officials – just in case you're going it alone.

Alternatively, let me note that you don't need a criminal finding in your favor to file civil litigation and win. Think of O.J.

Judges and arbitrators require only the facts, so don't bog their process down with emotions. Leave that mistake to the bad neighbors.

You have a strong chance of winning at this level if you are able to present the evidence I've recommended you gather, you have police witnesses who the judge might call on for endorsement of your charges, and your neighbor makes a damn fool of himself, which is likely because Neighbors From Hell just aren't very bright.

A win in municipal court sets the stage for litigation, and you can sue for various forms of suffering you've endured.

Meanwhile, exploit enemy weaknesses. Bad neighbors are often up to no good in other ways. Do they use drugs, cheat on their taxes, park illegally, drive without insurance, have a fake ID business on the side, or any other skeletons in the closet? Report any and all their misdeeds to authorities – consult your phone book's Blue Pages for ideas on who to call about what.

#10 – CONSIDER MEDIATION

Bad neighbors may refuse to participate in community mediation, available in more municipalities all the time, but many mediation groups are empowered to compel a party's participation; I haven't seen any with subpoena powers but that could come.

My concern with these groups is that they're composed of community citizens in the cases I've studied, and without a prosecutor on board there is less attention given to law than deserved. I worry that some mediation group members may have personal ties to the neighbor against whom the complaint is brought, and people don't always declare their conflicts of personal interest.

However, if using mediation, use it to your greatest advantage. Treat it as a legal case, have a lawyer represent you if possible, stick with facts and not emotions (except when articulating your suffering to connect with the mediation authority), and ask that the mediation conclude with a written agreement between you and the neighbor that costs him money for all future infractions of a definable nature. Money talks, especially if future parties or late-night dog-barking mean your neighbor has to pay, say, $100 or $250 to the mediation group or municipality (you'll still need proof in the form of audio-video evidence and/or a police call). Better yet, arrange for the neighbor to pay you for each successive disturbance – chronically noisy people rarely quiet down for more than a month at a time, so we should at least profit from their predictability.

#11 – TAKE A STAND AGAINST THE TIDE
Don't attend loud parties that would likely disturb neighbors, be there for good neighbors you know are having problems (keeping #8 above in mind), and raise your kids to be respectful of others – steer them clear of anti-neighbor influences, and don't involve them in conflicts you as an adult may be engaged in.

Again, neighbor disputes often present a sort of culture war, a contest over whose ways should prevail in a given community – those of the traditional, neighborly neighbor, or those of the Neighbors From Hell. The forces are stacked against the Good Neighbor Underclass, but preventive measures, a dose of diplomacy, and finally, knowing how to work the system to move it in our favor enable the good guys to win. And that's a turning of the tide that's long overdue.

Chapter 11: Serving Justice to the Neighbors From Hell

One of the things that most prevents good neighbors from triumphing over bad is our lack of knowing how to serve them the justice they so richly deserve. Correction, as just reviewed, covers a good deal of this. But not all.

While it's not possible to provide dead-on guidance here, there are some basics I'd like to highlight.

What laws are they breaking?

Police who seek minimal involvement in neighbor dispute resolution often ask NFH victims this very question, and we're frequently stumped. "Well, I had just swept the sidewalk in front of my house, and she came out and swept the leaves and dirt in front of her house onto my clean sidewalk," one might explain. Cops will laugh.

That's because there's no law on the books in most localities I've checked forbidding such rudeness. She didn't litter, technically, she didn't trespass, and she didn't make a terroristic threat.

Well, chances are good that a law *was* broken, but it requires some thought and ingenuity on our part to figure out which one. Hell, I wouldn't call the police if a neighbor simply swept her sidewalk and some debris landed on my property, even if it were just swept by me. Unless…

That neighbor did it in retaliation for my having called the police on her for noise or her loose pets or something else. Is vaguely-defined retaliation against a local ordinance? Most of the time, no.

But harassment often is. And if an otherwise non-illegal act is committed as part of a pattern of retaliation or other ongoing dispute, a harassment law being broken is provable.

However, police generally can't help with this. They'll come out and take a report from you, speak with the neighbor, and the report gets filed.

As explained earlier, it's then up to the NFH victim to file the harassment charge with the local court clerk (municipal, township or county). The clerk schedules a probable cause hearing, at which a judge listens to your evidence (consisting of tape recordings, a stack of police reports, your log of troubles over time, etc.) and hears the defense of the neighbor. He or she then determines whether the matter should go to trial.

If you bring the case without legal counsel, you might find it's hardly worth the effort. We ordinary people don't speak lawyer-talk, but judges do because they too are lawyers. If your neighbor hires a lawyer your case will be tossed out; opposing counsel will make mincemeat out of your case, making you look bad, poking holes in your evidence, and reinforcing the enemy, whose undeserved joy will eat away at your stomach lining.

So hire a lawyer if at all possible, to represent you in a criminal harassment claim you're bringing. While you're at it, depending on your lawyer's advice, consider bypassing the local criminal court process all together – a criminal finding in your favor is valuable, but particularly so if you're going to sue as a next step. Municipal judges don't like to send what they consider minor infractions to trial, especially if they're liberal judges who tend to associate neighbor complaints with conservative attitudes.

A criminal trial certainly poses great risk to your harassing neighbor, so again, heed counsel. Filing criminal charges may be a first step toward getting your neighbor to enter a legal agreement to cease all harassing activity, with monetary damages automatically awarded to you if he or she fails to comply with the agreement (the burden of proof would be on you in such a case).

Much as I'd like to outline every ordinance as it relates to neighbors, ordinances are local laws and there are millions of them. And most I've studied are inadequate for the protection of the Good Neighbor Underclass.

Nevertheless, do your diligence – get your hands on a copy of the local ordinances and zoning codes from your municipal authority or local library. Many municipalities have their laws available online, via their web site. Others provide this information via the Internet at whatever central code warehouse a municipality may choose; MuniCode.com and GeneralCode.com are two examples. If neither offers your locality's laws, search the Internet for "municipal codes on the internet" or search exhaustively for ordinances with the name of your town in the search field.

Make points against bad neighbors judiciously

After complaining to Mimi Cass about her dog's barking and getting nowhere, and finding my local police preferred to let Mimi be Mimi, I was on my own. Hiring a lawyer was not an option so soon after having to close a business and losing a lot of money.

I was lucky enough that our homes' layouts afforded me the capability of waking her household at 5 a.m., to make my point about her noise, without disturbing other neighbors. Use good judgment, and *don't exact a revenge that takes things further than necessary.*

For instance, in my view, Mimi Cass deserved being awakened overnight for the rest of her life for her years of recklessness concerning my household's peace and quiet, but that's my belief only because I'm angry. I say *be judicious* because our anger sometimes gets in the way of resolution.

Had I sounded our car alarms overnight every night for a week, two things would have happened. Mimi would have had more luck at getting me ticketed than I'd ever had in getting her ticketed (thanks mostly to her being a much more sympathetic character to police than I would ever be), and she would begin to learn that she faces my disturbance *no matter what she did* going forward.

By following up a late evening of her dog's barking with an early morning of our car alarms sounding, and *not* disturbing her when she did *not* disturb us, Mimi Cass's brain was able to slowly absorb the fact that her own attention to neighborliness translated into a benefit for her. Like Pavlov's dog, hearing car horns instead of bells.

Apply this to your own situation. Bad neighbors are the equivalent of very stupid children, and cannot be expected to learn neighborly behavior just because we want them to.

We need to be their teachers, their parents, their tough-love connection to the neighborhood around them. That's the thing about Neighbors From Hell. They cost us our time, our money and a good deal of our physical well-being. Serving them justice for our own sake stands to improve them while it diminishes us.

And sometimes, that's simply our best option.

Section III.

Appendices

Appendix 1: Moving from an NFH-Affected Home

Since good neighbors seldom have the time and refuse to devote the energy to deal with Neighbors From Hell, I realize that fighting the good fight is not for everyone, and many people choose instead to pick up their lives and seek a better neighbor experience elsewhere.

But there remains the matter of unloading your current home – positioned beside Neighbors From Hell – and there are things you should know if you own your home and wish to sell it.

The Seller's Property Disclosure (SPD) or similar document typically asks the seller to disclose, in writing above your legally binding signature, whether there have been any environmental issues that affect the home's livability. Can you feel your home's value dropping by about 20 percent if you're honest?

Of course you can, which is why many people don't disclose neighbor issues. Off these shores, you can face quite a lawsuit for failing to disclose such problems, and within the U.S. it is only a matter of time before some law firms devote their practice to litigation against sellers who dumped a tainted property on an unwitting buyer, who's now left holding the bottomless bag of the neighbor's dirty tricks.

Police reports and other documents are there for buyers to dig up, and I don't recommend lying on your SPD under any circumstance. Aside from your own culpability, it is morally wrong. But what to do? Who in their right mind wants to buy a home, knowing the hell you've just been through?

This is why we must immediately quash all tensions, as described earlier. This should be done well in advance of listing a home for sale, so that sufficient time elapses so that you can honestly pronounce there are no current neighbor issues; I say you should still disclose that there were problems in the past, but that they were resolved (if they were).

Remember, not all people will find your neighbors objectionable. I know for a fact that people who've bought my properties, where I had experienced problems, did not share my complaints (possibly because I'd corrected the neighbors before selling). As stated earlier, your Neighbor From Hell may be A-okay with me, and mine might not offend you one bit.

This is certainly the case where the issue is noise, as what constitutes a nuisance is "In the Ear of the Beholder." Issues of water run-off, drug and other criminal activity, and other more tangible complaints can present a different set of problems when you're selling. If you stay long enough to resolve them, the SPD statement of a past problem is not such a red flag for many potential buyers. However, unresolved problems certainly lower your home's value; if you want to get rid of your neighbor situation quickly, simply disclose these problems and take the hit to your asking price.

We learn again and again in life that it's not the act, but the cover-up that snags people. Having been the scene of neighbor issues does not make your home worthless to all buyers, but it may be *worth less*. Full disclosure of the facts – concerning past or present neighbor issues – may affect your sale, but won't come back to haunt you.

There are several recorded cases of this in the U.K., including one where a good neighbor who fought for a while and then moved on was successfully sued by her home's buyer for £15,000 for not revealing that she had a nuisance neighbor when selling her house.

Appendix 2: Advice for Landlords

Property owners would be well advised to prepare for potential disputes when signing new tenants. Get personal references -- not just a credit check. Ensure the lease specifies adherence to neighborly behaviors -- not just payment of the rent.

When a conflict emerges, be fair to find the best outcome. If it's tenant-vs.-tenant within one owner's property, an owner or manager can mediate to determine which party is wronging the other (often, both sides feel victimized by the other, but typically one side is truly egregious). The owner can adjust existing leases, getting signatures by lessees, as needed in order to ensure previously uncovered subjects get specified in the lease going forward, and landlords can use eviction to their advantage in order to protect the better tenant (the one most respectful of the property and its tenants). If the conflict is between a tenant and a neighbor outside the owned property, the landlord can speak with the neighbor or his/her landlord in an attempt to resolve the matter. If the complaint comes from outside about the landlord's tenant, the landlord should respond by promising, and then conducting, an investigation -- avoiding involvement in this case risks a lawsuit. The outcome of the investigation would determine how the landlord should proceed. If a tenant complains about an outside neighbor, the landlord should be mindful that a serious issue may make his/her property by definition unlivable, releasing a tenant from some terms of a lease and even making a tenant eligible for damages.

Anyone in authority when neighbors are in dispute should conduct himself/herself fairly, carefully and professionally, seeking legal counsel when in doubt. Dissatisfied parties can blog away and harm the reputation of an otherwise good property owner who fails to show an interest in protecting good tenants from bad neighbors.

Appendix 3: Loud as They Wanna Be

Because I admire Dennis Rodman's rise to success from unfortunate circumstances, I kind of hate to pick on him for being a Neighbor From Hell. But he is, or at least was. In the late 1990s, Newport Beach Police tell me they visited his home about 50 times in one year, due to noise complaints by neighbors. You and I think our neighbors are loud, but they probably have yet to land a helicopter out back. Additionally, he threw such huge bashes with hundreds of his friends and live bands (some rather famous like Liquid Soul, known for its album "Make Some Noise") that Newport Beach's helmeted police force would arrive by the dozen, sometimes summonsing the athlete-moviestar-author-Madonna lover, but never arresting him (not for his noisy parties, anyway).

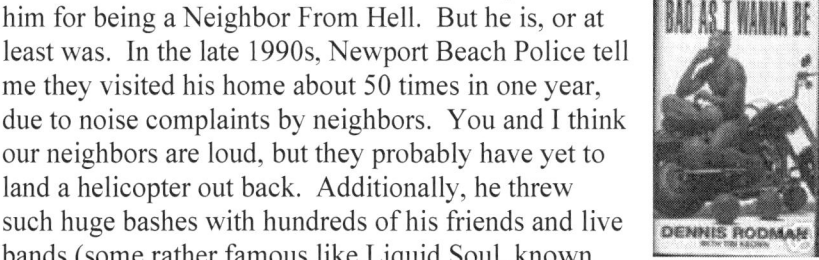

All he needed to do was show officers his compliance upon their arrival (even the fiftieth time taxpayers paid to have the force show up at his home for the same repeated offense), promise to keep it down, and he was off the hook. Until next time, when the cycle repeated, all the while driving his coastal community of decent neighbors crazy. Rodman is outspoken and even ran for political office out on the west coast to fight the new noise laws that were being strengthened because of his antics. And as much as we might like to see our noisy neighbors fined thousands of dollars for their offenses, The Worm could easily afford to write check after check. And he enjoyed popular media support...

> "... Often I've winced in anticipation of complaints from my neighbors during the countless hours my oldest son hammers out riffs and fills on his drums, or when his band shakes the walls of our garage with amplified guitar licks and crashing cymbals. But instead folks on an afternoon walk stop and listen in. 'He's really good,' some say. Others offer, 'It's nice you support his music.' Don't get me wrong. I enjoy a little peace and quiet as much as the next guy. But it nevertheless occurs to me that our ride on this rock is altogether short, too short to be complaining about the sounds of life. Too short to be hiding behind walls that grow ever higher. And too short, certainly, to be adding to the din by grousing about it."
>
> *- Daily Pilot columnist Byron de Arakal, June 27, 2001*

Rodman's not the only celeb to disturb his neighbors with nuisance noise. Sean Connery, Jim Belushi, Ann Curry, Paris Hilton, Bob Vila and many more have joined the ranks of Celebrity Neighbors From Hell. Curry and Vila upset New York neighbors with major construction projects, Connery and Hilton (who'd pair the two together?) with amplified music and other noise, and Jim Belushi battled neighbor Julie Newmar (the original Catwoman from the Batman series) over noise and other differences. The Belushi story actually ended rather well, as depicted in an ABC News 20/20 episode I contributed to about neighbor disputes. As Jim pointed out, importantly, having resolved the problems with neighbor Julie, "Now I have a friend, instead of an enemy."

Appendix 4: Meet the 'Boogie-Man' in Today's Tense Community

Dear Bob: A man has moved into the neighborhood that we know is on the sex offenders list. We want him out. What can we good neighbors do about these people moving into our community? There is no cure for pedophilia – these people should be castrated and locked up for life. Please advise.

– Anonymous

Actually, that man did give me his real, full name, but I don't want to embarrass him. Not to go into a George Carlin routine, but I am so very tired of today's hysterical suburban parents, who live in fear of anything and everything that might affect the well-being of their young children, who would be fine if they'd just choose not to let them roam so freely. I'm about to become a father myself at the late age of 42, and I will be watchful and probably a nervous wreck about my kids' safety no matter where we live.

And I am no defender of genuine sexual predators – I'm pretty conservative when it comes to criminals, especially those who victimize the innocent. Hurt a kid, an elderly person, a dog or cat and I personally won't miss you if you fry.

But did you know how easy it is to join the sex offenders list? You don't have to rape or sodomize a kid – you can be a 17-year-old boy having consensual sex with your 16-year-old girlfriend, and that's statutory rape. You can be a 22-year old guy touching yourself in your car in front of your own house, and that's indecent exposure if a cop shines his flashlight down onto your lap. And guess what these indiscretions lead to – a permanent stain that keeps you from getting a job, from being within a certain distance of children in your own family, and it makes you the boogie-man hiding in the closet of scared adults everywhere.

I fear the bad guys, I really do, but I'm not so quick to condemn people who are dubbed predators in a society so hell-bent on amalgamating in order to show up at the boogie-man's house – any boogie-man's house – with torches. So many of these people supposedly in fear are just jumping on a social bandwagon to fight against evil. We're too liberal in most law enforcement, yet we're extremely quick and harsh when the term sexual predator is used. I'm afraid of some fiend getting his hands on my future kids, but I have no fear that some kid who got laid or some 20-something with the poor enough judgment to play with himself outside the privacy of his home will ever prey upon the helpless, any more than someone not on The List.

The intention to keep children safe is pure, whether it's those who fought to expose the true criminals or those who don't want them living in their neighborhood. But do some research before going on a witch-hunt. I personally was accused of stalking the children of the friend of one of my own Neighbors From Hell. These friends of my neighbor were using their giant SUV to feign running me over while I walked my dog along the street in front of my house, and always sped off before I could catch their license number. So when I saw their kids playing nearby (I knew they were their kids because I'd seen them shouting obscenities up at my house with my neighbor's kids), I knew the SUV would be barreling by at some point, so I readied my video camera inside my living room window, and took my dog for a walk. Seeing the camera, and wanting to join the war against me that my neighbor had begun sucking them in to, they called the police and reported that I was videotaping their school-age children.

Well, at least I got the license plate number, and then could file a police report against them for harassment and filing a false claim (they allowed their kids to return to my house, unattended, later that day, to shout more obscenities, so how frightened were they I might hurt their kids?). But the fact remains that they could have taken their complaint, false or not, all the way. And in the small town in which I'm presently living, I could have found myself on The List.

So here's my advice. Predators are everywhere, and the ones you need to fear the most are the ones who aren't tainted by already being on a list of known offenders. The biggest sex offenders of children are members of their own family. Don't think you can rid your community of any and every threat to your kids, your property and yourself. Watch your kids – they're more likely to get hit by a speeding car down your suburban lane than to be abducted by the boogie-man.

Appendix 5: Co-ops for Us, Co-ops for Them

The concept of a co-op is that home buyers don't own their homes – they own shares in a corporation that owns their homes. Shareholders have a vote on who can and cannot live in their midst. Maybe this is separatist, but it keeps loud neighbors out.

The cooperative living concept may be the best way to go for people who choose not to live in the wilderness, but also don't want to deal with Neighbors From Hell. It's not fool-proof, but does offer more assurances to people buying a home that they can have a say about the behavior of the people they live among.

It's sometimes controversial. A co-op situation that might seem to stink of racism hails from Manhattan, where a co-op board in Barbara Streisand's building would not accept as her home's potential buyer, their potential new neighbor, Mariah Carey. Carey is a singer just like Streisand, but there's a difference. Granted, the co-op board is, very likely, Jewish or white, just like Barbara herself. Can it be that the board does not like Mariah because she's black, ambiguously so, but black nonetheless?

Probably not. Carey would not make for a bad neighbor because her Yiddish is lacking. Think about it. Who is Barbara Streisand going to have over for the evening? Barry Manilow? He's not likely to disturb residents of any color. Who's Mariah Carey going to be entertaining? Snoop-Dog, P-Diddy and other rappers lacking real names. Yes, they're all black. But if she were going to have Quincy Jones or Morgan Freeman over the board would not likely have been so distressed; in fact, either of those famous persons of color would likely be welcomed into Streisand's building, as a guest or resident. So it's not a matter of skin color, but one of behavior (and perhaps of age). Rappers and other young artists have marketed themselves to the point of cliché that they're "bad," they're gangstas, they're criminals. Maybe there wouldn't be a nightly shooting if Carey moved in, but there would certainly be loud noise, in the co-op board's view.

And that view is all that matters.

Prejudice, no matter how politically incorrect it may be as a word, is merely an ability to foresee, in some cases, what can be expected from a new neighbor. Streisand's co-op board wouldn't want Mariah Carey as a neighbor any more than Dennis Rodman would choose to live among so many "uptight" people complaining all the time. Were he in a co-op, he could have had a say in who his neighbors are.

143

Should all the world be made into co-ops? It may be unrealistic, and it's certainly separatist as an idea, but it could aid in keeping quiet people among other quiet people, loud among loud.

Appendix 6: *Entities* from Hell

It is not only who, but *what* neighbors us that can make a difference in quality of life in and around our homes. Some neighbors are not human – they're entities. In a "mixed-use community," one combining residential zoning with business and entertainment, entities can cause a good deal of harm

Noisy entities of any sort – airports, shopping centers, amusement parks and the like – make it difficult for those who don't want their human Neighbors From Hell to get away with noise. Many areas now use decibel measuring devices to gauge the level of noise being made by a neighbor when the complaint evolves into police and other authority involvement. *Those devices are calibrated outside, meaning that your neighbors can be noisier inside their homes and yards, by law, if the natural surrounding sound is abnormally loud.* Their TVs can be louder, their backyard party's DJ can turn it up louder, and their barking dog gets away with higher volume as well.

People go to war with neighboring entities when they present problems to the community. Examples would be polluting factories, nuisance bars and planned shopping centers. What neighbors us matters, mostly because we're protective of our neighborhoods when it comes to outsiders.

A nuisance bar, for example, seldom serves the community immediately surrounding it. Bars that cater to nearby residents usually don't produce a 2 a.m. exodus of loud drunks who pee on the street, hop on Harleys and set off car alarms as they speed home in an intoxicated blitz. "Local bar" patrons depart more quietly, generally speaking, and walk home. This is, after all, their neighborhood. The bar itself is not so much the problem. It's a building filled with liquor, owned by someone who's making a living (often a very nice living that easily affords fines). It's the people. Community residents are weary of outsiders with good cause.

Crowds and mob mentality are a growing problem. More and more people seem to live for chaotic hullabaloo events like Mardi Gras, ethnic parades and picnics, sports team playoffs and New Year's Eve. They seem to need allowance to let loose and be crazy, defining fun in ways that cost those around them. And, when area residents affected by their antics speak out, they're deemed uptight.

On the opposite end of the nuisance entity spectrum is a church, and yes, churches can make for bad neighbors. I find that, particularly in urban areas, churches create disturbances not on Sunday mornings but during the rest of the week. Saturday weddings bring traffic-blocking limousines with youthful partiers hanging out the sunroof screaming and spilling their beers. Weeknights draw non-neighbors to church parking lots, fields and playgrounds, and they tend to respect the immediate community as much as bar revelers do.

Church bells make noise, which has grown more objectionable with technology, just as have other forms of noise. The quaint Sunday morning bell being rung by a parishioner has been replaced by amplified organ music that resounds throughout the neighborhood all day. And no, it's not for everyone, but worse is the way in which it raises the natural noise level of a community.

I consulted with a woman in California whose neighbor across the street was a church that played loud amplified music; she complained to church leaders to no avail, and then involved the police who told her churches are exempt from the local noise ordinance.

Now that's power. Nuisance bars have the money to pay the fines, but churches don't even need to face penalties. So, this woman became an ordained minister through an online course, and began blasting her own music out her window for church-goers to hear.

The church leaders called the police and the police shut her down. Being a minister doesn't make one's home a church, of course, but you have to admire her spunk.

Online Counsel Transcripts
Here are samples from online counsel I've provided via NeighborSolutions.com. Names and some details have been changed to protect good neighbors.

Dear Bob,

It's ironic that your site is called Neighbor from Hell as the neighbor causing me grief is in fact the Catholic Church. Let me explain. My house abuts the playing field of a church and school. I've lived here for some eight years, alas I bought the place and each year the noise situation gets more annoying. Not annoying like a buzzing mosquito but stress and anxiety inducing annoying. I fully expected that grade school kids would be playing there during school hours but as of late I've had to contend with marauding soccer players (mostly illegal aliens) who have co-opted the field after hours and on weekends. I have been in touch with the police and even got a call from sergeant saying that he'd spoken with head priest and that priest said he can't control this stuff (in essence). The sarge basically said to give them a call and they'd chase them away. I gave up doing this after calling twice to no avail. The switchboard operator sounds irritated when I call and it's really demoralizing to feel like I'm the one doing the annoying! Anyway, what is most irritating and jarring is the kicking of the ball. It sounds like a car door slamming again and again. I can hear it indoors with doors and windows shut and it is seriously making me a nervous wreck. I find myself, on some level just *waiting* for it to come. Weekends are the pits. And being in my own yard is just impossible, front or back. I consider myself reasonable. Oh, local ordinances do nothing for me. I was going to investigate state law. I really don't have the resources for a lawyer at this point and am deeply troubled that I'll never sell the place. Believe me, if I could move I would. My neighbors are parishioners and have been unsympathetic. You know there is an old Brazilian adage that basically says that pepper on someone else's ass doesn't burn. I've called the rectory once or twice and left message on the machine. No response. Honestly, where has common courtesy gone? I thought of sending a certified letter but am just confused and unsure of how to proceed. I've even tried visualizing the problem away!! Feel sort of undermined by all parties involved including police. Really don't what else to do, I do know I'm getting sicker each day. Incidentally, there is a soccer field in the public park half a block away.

from Florida

147

Dear Florida,

I like the Brazilian adage you cited. I'd keep calling the police, ignoring any irritation in the voice of the switchboard operator/dispatcher. Have others call, even if from cell phones from elsewhere (just call friends and ask them to call to complain). Numerous complaints result in better police action. Too bad we need to do this, but low priority response forces us.

Speak with the head priest or whomever else is in charge there. Churches can be miserable neighbors, I've found, and they're difficult to fight. Be as diplomatic as you can be -- priests don't fear local law enforcement, lawsuits or anything like that. A drop in flock numbers would concern them, and you could imply that others in the neighborhood are equally disturbed but don't wish to complain. I'd press them to shut down the field (is it gated?) when not reserved by legitimate parishoners; remind them the soccer players have nearby alternatives.

Dear Bob,

I found your webpage and have a question.

Can you recommend an attorney who can help me file suit against a restaurant/bar business establishment that is placing live bands on their outside deck on weekends where music is played until 2am in a quiet lake community.

There is no noise ordinance in the village or the county. The lake community has an association with officers/board members. These people seem to be taking the position that there is nothing they can do to stop the noise.

from Nevada

Dear Nevada,

I don't have a lawyer in your area I can recommend, but I suggest you look for a larger firm, because these carry more weight when going up against big establishments. This bar is likely making enough money to defend itself vigorously.

You do need an ordinance on the books, and if you and several of your neighbors begin a grassroots effort you can get one in place (but that will take at least six months). If enough people are being disturbed, your association should act on your behalf -- gather a group and rally at their next meeting.

Build a committee of neighbors and seek advice from a county or state official, and local police, to help in designing a law modeled for your town. Visit www.NoiseFree.org for ideas there and other support.

But first, approach the establishment's management about the problem if you haven't yet.

Appendix 7: NFH Syndrome in the News

Stories like this aren't all that unusual any more. News coverage seldom tells the whole story, and often many details are just dead wrong. So always be careful about who you conclude is the real Neighbor From Hell when you see and read stories like this one from the *Charlotte Observer* web site:

> **Feud ends in gunfire: 1 killed, 4 hurt**
> *By Cleve R. Wootson Jr. and Steve Lyttle*
> *Posted: Friday, May 29, 2009*
>
> A simmering feud between next-door neighbors and a fight over a dog ended with one person dead and four injured Wednesday night in Caldwell County.
> Neighbors and authorities say Rolland Younce's pit bull attacked and killed a neighbor's cat. The neighbor responded by shooting the dog, authorities said. Younce then shot the neighbor and his 8-year-old daughter, authorities said.
> Younce also allegedly shot two deputies before dying in a shootout with authorities.
> His body was found near his trailer, on Grandin Road off N.C. 18, about 12 miles north of Lenoir.
> The neighbor and his daughter were hospitalized with serious injuries, authorities said Thursday. They were identified as Tony Moore and his daughter Ashley, a student at nearby Kings Creek Elementary. The deputies – Marty Robbins and Thomas McManus – were less severely injured.
> Amy Moore told WCNC-TV that she got two calls Thursday afternoon. The first was from her husband, saying he'd shot the neighbor's dog while it was on the porch. The second call, from her daughter, came after the shooting.
> "She said that daddy was sitting in the yard bleeding," Moore said.
> Younce and the Moores had been feuding for several years, said Tammie Roberts, whose

backyard bumps up against the land of both families.

The neighbors had argued over the property line since Younce moved in. Accusations flew about wood reportedly stolen from a recently completed fence.

Two years ago, Roberts said, Younce's pit bull bit Moore's children. It's still unclear whether authorities did anything about the dog, but Roberts said Moore once approached her about joining a civil lawsuit. She declined, reluctant to get involved in her neighbors' squabble.

Their arguments continued, sometimes ending violently.

"The law has been down here I don't know how many times," Roberts said, "and this isn't the first time shots have been fired here."

Roberts said she was on good terms with the Moores and Younce, and even with his dog. The pit bull wasn't vicious with her, but it sometimes got loose, including Wednesday night when Roberts and her boyfriend got home about 10:30.

It performed a few tricks for them that night, including lying on the ground, and Roberts said her boyfriend considered taking it back to Younce's house.

"I said, 'No,'" Roberts said. "I was afraid of getting involved in their fight."

Police were called to the scene about a half-hour after that to deal with a dispute over an animal, the sheriff's office said.

Caldwell County Sheriff Alan Jones said Robbins, the first deputy who responded, was shot as he approached the Moores' house.

A second deputy, McManus, arrived moments later and also was shot. They returned fire at the shooter and were pulled to safety when three other deputies arrived.

At that point, Jones said, the sheriff's office set up a perimeter around the area, called in the SWAT team and requested help from other departments.

Jones said the SWAT team was able to reach the Moore family and pull them to safety. They also began a search for the shooter.

Younce was found dead in his yard from a gunshot wound, Jones said, adding that it wasn't self-inflicted.

Ashley Moore was flown to Wake Forest University Baptist Hospital in Winston-Salem. Her mother said she was in intensive care, with gunshot wounds to her liver, kidney and lung.

Her father was hospitalized at Carolinas Medical Center, but his condition was not available.

Robbins was hospitalized at Carolinas Medical Center with gunshot wounds to the arm and leg. He was released from the hospital Friday morning. McManus was shot in the arm and treated at Caldwell Memorial Hospital in Lenoir.

Neighbors got calls from the sheriff's office about midnight telling them to stay away from windows and turn out lights. Roberts said her family stayed crouched in the dark in an inside hallway for most of the night.

"This has been going on for years – them bickering back and forth," she said. "This is something that could have been prevented. … It didn't have to end that way."

Appendix 8: Harassment

Although so much of this book includes discussion of harassment, I'm including this appendix for one reason:

Every neighbor dispute that evolves into police calls, lawsuits and even my involvement, has involved it in some form.

It's not that the legal definition of harassment is met in all cases, but at least one party feels harassed in the dispute, often as a result of bringing to someone's attention their un-neighborly ways and then facing the consequential wrath of the Neighbor From Hell.

But bad neighbors increasingly feel harassed, too. Receiving notes, having to deal with police and other authorities coming to visit them, and unfriendliness toward them by we who consider ourselves the "good guys," all can be considered harassment by the person on the receiving end.

Harassment is defined locally by municipal ordinance, and sometimes alternatively or additionally by county and/or state law.

To file a harassment charge, you can't just *feel* harassed; your treatment by another person or persons must fit the legal definition. Your local police, library, prosecutor's office or court clerk can provide a written definition, and often can hear your story and provide guidance as to how to proceed.

Civil law is a much wider arena when it comes to going after jerks for their jerky behavior. While this may seem encouraging to the Good Neighbor Underclass, so underserved by authorities and legal systems, I believe a backlash could be in store.

Less intelligent people who exhibit un-neighborly behaviors can hire lawyers, often just as easily as we can. And their lawyers can pile on to the misery already being dumped on us by bad neighbors. We're not the only ones who can use the law to our benefit – in fact, bad neighbors are using legal retaliation against those who bring them complaints more all the time, in my research.

So let me state again that writing notes, leaving voicemail, sending email, posting various Internet messages and other methods of putting on record any communication with a problem neighbor, exposes us to criminal and civil retaliation.

The only written material coming from you and going to your Neighbor From Hell should be official complaints through authorities and letters through your lawyer. And even these can be construed as harassing.

It's also important to remember that actions and behaviors by people with whom we have a negative history might *feel* like harassment even when they're not bona fide *legal* harassment. That's because the intent of the action and behavior is aimed at bothering us. We know this.

And, when we react to it, however right and righteous we may be, we're sometimes doing ourselves a disservice. Again, informing Neighbors From Hell of precisely how they can get under our skin may as well be an invitation to continue the behavior. Remember, they're jerks. Give them no further ammunition.

Online Counsel Transcripts
Here are samples from online counsel I've provided via NeighborSolutions.com. Names and some details have been changed to protect good neighbors.

Dear Bob,
We have a vacation home at a lake. We spend a good deal of our time there even though it's not our main home. A new neighbor moved in right after we moved in. At first he and his wife seemed very nice - even normal. Now I realize that we have a man with psychological issues as a neighbor. He is constantly trespassing on our property. He tries to control how we landscape, when we do it, and how much we do. Since we are not there full time we try to stay on top of the mowing and weed-whacking. When we have extra time, we do tree trimming and property improvements. The other neighbors in the neighborhood have complimented us for improving the property. In addition to constant nagging, nosiness and complaining to us, he has a dog that roams around loose and poops everyday in our yard instead of his own. There is a leash law in our county but he ignores it.

We are trying to avoid any contact with him but recently he confronted us at the property line, cussed us out for not removing our TV antennae which was there before we bought the place.

The antenna is legal and would be costly for us to remove since it is a large tower. It isn't the prettiest thing in the world but we aren't in any hurry to get rid of it. He said that if we didn't comply with his wishes we would be very sorry. We called the sheriff since it sounded like a threat. The sheriff told him to not talk to us and for us not to talk to him. In order to keep his dog off our property we would like to have a fence but it would be very costly to us.

This vacation home was a longtime dream of ours but now it has become a nightmare because of the nosy neighbor. We would like to do many improvements and enhancements but would like to do it at our own pace and discretion not as a ruling from a neighbor. If we give in to this bully, there will be no end to this harassment.

We don't know what to do. We are thinking about just selling the place and forget about our dream of retiring there.

from Texas

Dear Texas,

Don't sell. I handle these disputes numerous times each day, and yours is not severe. While he is unpleasant, he hasn't directly threatened you, and the law has shown its support for your side. You have plenty going for you here.

Keep making your improvements at your own pace. Do the antenna last if you'd like, but only if you'd like -- not to be spiteful (I understand the temptation, believe me). Maintain your relationships with all the good neighbors, and be careful not to complain about this guy to the others. Our better neighbors don't want to become involved in such conflicts and may perceive you to be negative or intolerant if you complain too much.

Take photos/video of the dog on your property and gather evidence of any other wrongdoing of the neighbor's. File a charge with the Alba court clerk (or whatever jurisdiction handles this by you) for either harassment, property damage, pet nuisance or any other applicable charge. Present your evidence to the judge and see if the guy doesn't just stop bothering you.

Meanwhile, obey the sheriff, and document any events of the neighbor's disobedience, preferably on video. Lawmen don't like when their advice isn't heeded, and your neighbor will likely violate the order to stay away from you soon enough. Keep me informed.

Dear Bob,

    I am having a big problem with my neighbor. I bought my house two years ago. Six months after I moved in the trouble started. My neighbor who happened to move in about 6 months before I did started calling the police over and over. These calls involved our snow blowing of our driveway, with the snow blowing towards his house.

    There were three calls to the police in one afternoon while we were having a cookout with my family – the complaint was loud music. The best was him calling because there were footprints in the snow – he wanted the police to take pictures and arrest the four-year-old child who'd left them. He has made over 80 complaints. Not once was I given a warning because when the cops came they found nothing to be true. He has called and made complaints when no one was at home or in the middle of the night when all lights were out. I have received no help from the police or the city.

    He then put no trespassing signs all over his property. The other neighbors who have lived in their homes for 30-40 years are so upset. They have come over when the police showed up and told them he was lying. The city will not do a thing about it. We have gone to four council meetings and complained along with eight of my neighbors. Nothing was done. He then put video cameras pointed directly into the bedrooms of my 16-year-old and myself. I called the police, made complaints, and they finally after two months made him take them down. Needless to say my daughter will not get dressed in her bedroom anymore.

    Two other neighbors caught him videotaping the front of my home in the middle of the night, outside my daughter's window. They called the police and they told them there is nothing they can do. They sit two feet outside of my bedroom window in their chairs with a fire going just staring into my window. There is much more too much to write in an email.

    I worked my butt off to buy my home and enjoy my yard and my family coming over to visit. This neighbor has destroyed everything that I worked to get. I have gone to see a couple of lawyers and they tell me the same thing, that it is hard to sue because they have not caused any property damage. They are willing to do it if I fork over a lot of money. I live on one income and barely make it on that. If I do fork out the money then I am at risk at losing my house because I can't afford the payment and pay for a lawyer.

I have tried every avenue and I keep running into a brick wall. This is a bully trying to intimidate me and my family. My son moved out last October and every time he comes over he gives my son the finger or stares him down.

I don't sleep. I hear noises and I am up the rest of the night. My work performance has gone downhill because all I think about is this. I cannot afford to sell – believe me, if I could I would be gone. He recently had a survey done and sent me a letter from an attorney telling me to remove my driveway and my fence from his property.

I need some honest and serious advice. I don't know what to do or who to turn to for help. I have called every person in the City and they just talk to me like I am an idiot. They have admitted they let this go too far and now it is out of their hands. What the heck does that mean? I called the news and they tell me to call the police. The police tell me to call a lawyer and the lawyer tells me to call the mayor. I am running in circles. Any help that you can suggest would be greatly appreciated.

from Ohio

Dear Ohio,

What may have prompted this situation? Is there excessive noise coming from your home? Does your neighbor do this to others?

Right off the bat, I suggest you and your daughter take a self-defense training class, as it builds self esteem where it's been lost, and lets off steam. It's good for other members of the household as well.

But I'm still intrigued as to your neighbors' motives.

Ohio replied:

I have no idea what prompt the situation. Everyone seems to think he has done this before. We do not make excessive noise, nothing more then everyday living. I have a teenager and her friends jumping on the trampoline in the backyard having a good time in the middle of the afternoon is as loud as it gets around here. Honestly, we have given him no motive for any of this. I have tried to ignore the burden that he has placed on us. That seems to give him more reason for disturbing our privacy and taunting us.

Thanks for listening to me vent. It helps, believe it or not.

I wrote back:

Teens on a trampoline can create a great deal of noise disturbance. Move or permanently remove the trampoline and cut off all contact with the neighbor.

I would bet the tramp noise set off his behavior toward you and your family, and while his reaction seems harsh, and may constitute harassment, police can't help you much because he is not breaking a law if he has genuine complaints.

Getting rid of the trampoline, not playing music outside or creating any noise disturbance will disable your neighbor from filing any legitimate complaints about noise.

The letter directing you to move your driveway and fence seems not-so-serious to me – your neighbor may have directed his attorney to scare you, and few things are as scary as the threat of litigation when you can't afford to defend yourself, I know. I would not respond to this letter, but if a second comes, you'll want legal representation.

Since you can't afford it, I'd look into local law schools with legal aid projects where future lawyers defend you. Alternatively, larger and mid-size law firms do take on *pro bono* work (representing you without charging you), and neighbor cases are increasingly interesting to real estate lawyers and litigators who are looking to specialize in neighbor law. Finding a pro bono attorney would take some calling around.

Appendix 9: Teaching kids to be Better Neighbors

Reporter Shera Dalin spoke with me in composing the following article excerpt aimed at kids, which ran on TheFreeLibrary.com.

Be a good neighbor:
Learn to get along with those who live nearby

Why should you care about being a nice neighbor? For starters, you'll feel good about helping someone else. But there's more, as Juan Mundo-Sifuentes can tell you. When he applied for a scholarship, [his next-door neighbor's] mom wrote a glowing recommendation letter. Mundo-Sifuentes won the scholarship to help pay for his first year at the University of Missouri-Columbia.

"If you're a great neighbor, I'm certainly going to do everything I can to help you," says Bob Borzotta, a board member of the Anti-Violence Partnership of Philadelphia. "[For example,] if I am influential in the business community, I can help young people get jobs. ... You scratch my back, I'll scratch yours."

Stephen Sundet, 18, remembers a couple of older neighbors he used to help regularly before his family moved from Cleveland Heights, Ohio. He painted their houses, mowed their lawns, and shoveled their snow. It made him feel good, and they returned his kindness: One neighbor treated Sundet and his brothers to a baseball game, and another took him to see the Cleveland Browns play football.

But special favors aren't the reason to treat those around you well; being a good neighbor is its own reward. "My neighbors are like a second family to us," Sundet says. "We still remain close to our old neighbors even though we do not get to see them every day."

Stepping Up

That cohesiveness doesn't always come easy, though, notes Borzotta. "We're all not getting along so well anymore," he says. "People are not thinking of others."

Being a good neighbor means being responsible and considerate of others. Did your baseball break someone's window? Apologize and offer to pay for it. Planning a wild dance party? Keep the music down, and be polite if neighbors complain.

Many times, teens don't realize what they're doing bothers others, because neighbors may be reluctant to criticize children, says Borzotta. For instance, a group of teens just hanging out can sometimes intimidate adults. Adults often gripe that teens play music too loud or are rowdy, while teens may complain that adults don't want to hear their side of a situation.

Despite your best efforts to be considerate, some members of your community might seem to be in a permanent state of grumpiness. Try to be kind or understanding. You never know what they might be dealing with: an illness, money problems, loneliness, or other issues. Compassion can be a powerful remedy. In the course of your life, you might have neighbors you just can't find a way to get along with; by acting civil and respectful now, you'll learn how to minimize tension and problems later.

Good Neighbors, Good Communities

By accepting your neighbors, quirks and all, you'll discover the benefits of being connected. "When neighbors know and trust one another, the community is better able to prevent crime, to monitor children, and to accomplish shared goals, like keeping a park clean and fun," says David J. Harding, assistant professor of sociology at the University of Michigan. In other words, we're all in this together.

Being a good neighbor doesn't stop with the people who live adjacent to you. It applies to your entire community, explains Dennis Kahl, a community development educator with the University of Nebraska-Lincoln Extension in Seward County. He works with youth to teach them community leadership skills. For example, kids in rural David City, Neb., were bored because there was little to do. Under a leadership program Kahl organized, a group of a dozen young people started talking to the town's leaders about establishing a youth center. That discussion opened a deeper level of respectful dialogue and made the adults aware of the teens' needs.

You can make an impact not only in your neighborhood, but in your community. When you offer to organize block parties, pitch in to clean up local trails, or serve on your town's youth commission or teen advisory board, you help make the place you live better for everyone. And that makes you a good neighbor.

Good Neighbor Gestures
1. Treat people the way you want to be treated.
2. Respect public and private property. If damage occurs, own up to your role in it and do whatever you can to put things right.
3. Keep the noise levels down. Would you want to hear your neighbor's music at full blast?
4. Be kind and courteous, even if a neighbor is grumpy or mean.
5. Share your skills and time with others who live around you. Visit an elderly neighbor. Pick up litter. Help someone learn to ride a bike. Look out for the younger neighborhood kids. Volunteer to shovel a neighbor's driveway or mow his or her lawn.

Appendix 10: The Happy Ending

A producer with the Rachael Ray show wanted me to come on with two neighbors who were at war, but with my help, are now best buddies.

I explained that neighbor dispute resolution doesn't work that way, that each side is typically satisfied, if ever, to have no further business with the other – no disturbances or infractions, no complaints, no "nothing."

You look past them if you happen upon them, and they look past you. No, this doesn't seem so great, but this is what passes for a happy ending in today's neighborhood where disputes over the seemingly smallest things snowball into hard-fought long-lived wars.

Dealing with Neighbors From Hell, as I said earlier, is more a matter of ongoing conflict management. Situations don't often end or become rosy without one party moving away or being struck by lightning.

Still, the concept interests me. Could people at war become friends? Would I be receptive of an old enemy coming to me with the desire to patch things up? Would any bad neighbor I've had be so receptive?

I don't have an answer. I know that some NFH situations have been averted, and some have been resolved to the victim's liking. But for all parties to join hands and sing a happy song?

It worked for Jim Belushi and Julie Newmar. But that's in the world of show business and Hollywood happy endings.

In the real world, I'll take just plain-old *being* happy. NFH experiences leave us miserable, agitated, suspicious toward current and future neighbors, and generally upset with the world. Personal happiness is far from the emotional ruin left in the wake of conflict close to home, even years after the war ended or subsided, or the parties were parted by someone's decision to move away. Coming back to life isn't a snap.

Our brains get weighed down from neighbor conflict, to the point that chemicals literally aren't jumping from Side A to Side B – necessary for us to feel joy and be ourselves.

There is nothing wrong with seeking therapy and taking a prescribed medication to repair the damage. I've found it helpful for myself, and I hear good results from others.

We have to abandon the unhealthy outlets that we somehow find useful when dealing with a neighbor war. We find ourselves hating them and self-medicating with everything from alcohol to caffeine. We come to blame our bad neighbors for robbing us of our happiness, when in fact, no one has taken anything away from us – we gave it up of our own accord.

Having healthy outlets is better. Self-defense training classes, workouts, tai-chi, yoga, regular walks in the neighborhood, community advocacy and volunteering – such activities effectively wipe the webs from our eyes, get our hearts pumping and our brains thinking positively, and rebuild our diminished sense of self and self-esteem. Above all, find good neighbors, be good to them, and seek pleasure out and about in your community.

What we need is a whole new mindset, to undo the damage and return to our normal selves. I heard a quote the other day: "Never underestimate your ability to change yourself, and never overestimate your ability to change others." It applies to our NFH situations. The misery becomes too familiar, and we become indoctrinated to start our days with negativity. Most people, without some form of therapy or faith or other positive influence, cannot readily stop the negative thought processes and begin more positive ones.

It applies equally to the concept many of us have about our problem neighbors. We think early on that we can change them with pleasantness, or directness, or harshness. We later believe we can rely on others like our better neighbors, law enforcement, landlords, community advocates and so forth, to solve our neighbor problems for us. But the only change we can effectively make is in our minds, where so much agony has been endured for long enough. We're not going to forever change bad neighbors into good ones – we'll just manage the conflict situations bad ones present for us.

We mustn't blame ourselves for missteps we've taken up to this point, which have in some cases worsened the situation, and which so often have caused us deeper angst.

Being immersed in a serious dispute with a neighbor isn't just a drag. It does physical and emotional damage. That needs to be undone in order for us to turn the page and get back into life.

Made in the USA
Lexington, KY
21 September 2011